Love and Ecstasy

ALSO BY ARTHUR AND LIBBY COLMAN

Pregnancy: The Psychological Experience (1971)

LOVE AND ECSTASY

Arthur D. Colman, M.D.
AND
Libby Lee Colman, PH.D.

A Continuum Book
THE SEABURY PRESS - NEW YORK

The Seabury Press
815 Second Avenue
New York, N.Y. 10017

Designed by Nancy Dale Muldoon
Printed in the United States of America

LIBRARY OF CONGRESS CATALOGING IN PUBLICATION DATA

Colman, Arthur D 1937–
Love and ecstasy.

(A Continuum book)
1. Interpersonal relations. 2. Love. I. Colman, Libby Lee, joint author. II. Title.
HM132.C624 152.4 75-2136
ISBN 0-8164-9250-6

Contents

Preface

AT times this book seems to us quite new and original; at other times we realize how derivative much of it really is. The subject of love is timeless; but our sources and examples are drawn from the past as well as the present. Nor can we begin to name all the people, events, books, and ideas that have contributed to its making, for love is something all-pervading. The writing of this book called, directly or indirectly, on the total knowledge and experience of us both. Much of our material is technical and complex, but we have limited footnotes and acknowledgements for the sake of clarity. Our students, patients, and friends may recognize parts of themselves in some of the illustrative material, but in general the case histories are composites and not of any one person. Finally we owe a debt of gratitude to those anonymous friends who gave us permission to quote directly from their autobiographies.

The English language has no comfortable solution to sexist labels, for it has no neutral singular pronoun. It would have been awkward and intellectually limiting to refer throughout to abstract male and female persons in the plural, so we often talk about a single person as "he." In the developmental section, "she" generally refers to the parenting figure, "he" to the infant. We acknowledge the reality of male parents and female infants, but succumb to stylistic considerations. Generally we use illustrations for both sexes.

We have not included a special section on homosexual love despite its importance, though we believe our analysis of dyadic experience applies equally to homosexual and heterosexual pairs. Our concern is with *ecstatic* orientation, not sexual orientation. Our own identity, our dyadic "we," is male/female. That identity inevitably has had some influence on our perspective, but we have tried to be sensitive to problems specific to both sexes as well as to those which transcend sexual identity.

As with our earlier book, *Pregnancy: The Psychological Experience*, the writing of this one served as a powerful experience of renewal for each of us as individuals and in our relationship with each other. We hope it will also enrich our readers by clarifying their own understanding of their personal experiences with love and ecstasy alone, in groups, and most of all with those special persons whom they love.

I

A Definition of Love

THIS book is about love. It does not presume to treat the subject comprehensively, for love is too vast and elusive to deal with as a whole. Rather it establishes a definition which limits, if not love itself, the aspects of love to be discussed here. This definition places love at the intersection of two planes, one experiential, the other relational: *love is the experience of ecstasy in an interpersonal relationship.*

Both ecstasy and relationships are universal to the human condition. They are rooted in our biology and our society. We possess a neurophysiological "pleasure center" which underlies the potential for ecstasy throughout our lives. Every culture has special social institutions designed to activate and shape the forms of ecstatic experience. Similarly, relationships are essential to our biological survival and personal development. All cultures have social institutions designed to facilitate and delimit patterns of relating with others.

The above definition emphasizes the experience and the relating, while not restricting the object, of love. It allows for such diverse phenomena as love of family, love of group, love of nation, love of God, and love of humanity. The central concern, however, is with love for a single Other, with the variety of ecstatic experience possible between two people in a profound relationship.

The two-person relationship is the keystone to human linkage. Through pairing, men and women seek to escape their essential loneliness and spiritual isolation, to find immortality through offspring, to further their material well-being, and to discover personal joy. Two people bonded together in a profound relationship create a dyad, a unit of two, a new form made up of its parts, yet greater than the simple sum of the two separate beings.

For each of us, life begins in the basic mother/infant dyad. We are totally bonded to, even contained within, our mothers. We discover ecstasy and learn to relate from within this dyad. Gradually, we separate ourselves from the maternal shelter and learn to have ecstatic experience and intimate relationships elsewhere. We begin to participate in other dyads and to love in other forms, alone and in groups. Eventually we may establish a primal man/woman dyad, a union with another adult of the opposite sex with whom we recreate the original dyad through procreation. This is our fundamental life cycle, which we share with many other life forms. We frequently extend the boundaries of this limited cycle and create other kinds of relationships, other envelopes for ecstatic experience. We form same-sexed pairs, we link together in groups, we seek ecstasy in isolation, we live beyond the birth cycle itself, liberated from biological imperatives and free to create any of the forms of ecstatic relationship we choose.

As we search for ecstatic experience and struggle to relate effectively with others, we develop individual patterns and preferences. The forms of love are myriad, but the choices of any particular individual are not totally open. Each of us evolves a style of loving uniquely his own. That style has been shaped not only by the ways in which we make use of ecstatic experiences and relationships, but also by the constraints each of us feel in our need for dependency.

The conditions of our childhood development make us as bound to the pursuit of human security as we are to the pursuit of biological sustenance. We need others. We depend on them for emotional, physical, and social support. Dependency is the psychological analogue to physical need. For the adult, much like the child, most meaningful relationships begin by satisfying both dependency and ecstasy, but the vicissitudes of living fragment and disassociate one from the other.

For most of us, particularly during times of insecurity, our essential human aloneness takes precedence over our quest for ecstasy. We all have the ecstatic capacity for merger with another, but we also have a need for the Other to be available to us. There are worlds beyond dependency for individuals who are committed to a total sharing love with each other—the incredible joys of intimacy, sexual profundity, intertwined personal knowledge—but to love fully in a long-term relationship and to reach a plateau where ecstatic union is an ongoing potential also requires the satisfaction of one's need for dependency.

The wish to be cared for is often taken to be love, but may actually be love's central antagonist. There are immense problems in developing an enduring relationship in which ecstatic experience is integrated with daily living. *In pure form, relationships move toward dependence; ecstasy moves toward isolation. Melding the two in a continuous love experience is a supreme creative act.*

Each of us becomes aware of love for another in brief, intense moments. Love peaks and then passes. Rarely can it be continuously experienced, for the traffic of our daily lives distracts us from the ecstasy of our relationship with another. We seem to acknowledge the peak moments of love as a great good, as something that gives meaning to life and brings us our most exquisite pleasures, but we are at the same time distrustful of its reality. We think of love as something that just happens, as "made in heaven" or as "chemistry," implying it is magical and out of control. We rarely think of love as something requiring work or discipline. We adore romantic fairy tales, but do not really believe in the "happily ever after." In our cynicism, most of us would admit that it is just as well Romeo and Juliet died young, for we assume their passion could not have sustained itself through the realities of marriage. We read novels and newspaper articles about individuals who throw over a career or a marriage for a powerful love, but we fear and distrust anyone who tries it in real life.

We value the peaks and yet we assume that they are transient. We say we should marry for love, but we do not really believe that emotion can be worked on, developed, or maintained. We have no love discipline parallel to our mystical disciplines. Once past the initial "enlightenment" of falling in love, we have no Way to chart an ongoing path leading into new realms of ecstatic merger with a single Other.

Nevertheless our culture is actively experimenting with new forms of social units to achieve more meaningful relationships. Currently there is a variety of "open" marriages in which each partner may take on transient lovers while remaining loyal to his primary family group. Or we try "group" marriage in which each individual has an array of intense lovers without a basic attachment to any. The hope is that love, like household duties, might be reasonably distributed among the members of the group, as if to sidestep the difficulties of encompassing passion and fidelity. However, human relationships inevitably involve power struggles, pecking orders, and possessiveness. The experimenters frequently find themselves facing the very emotions they had hoped to avoid.

Not surprisingly, we are also experimenting with keeping love alive through the modern magic of technology. Since the time of Freud, an intimate relationship with another has been at the heart of psychotherapeutic techniques used to understand human nature. Gradually, the task of analyzing a relationship over an extended time has shifted to more simplified techniques that deal little with the quality of relationships. We have temporary groups in which we can explore problems of intimacy with anonymous people who will never enter our daily lives. We have dedicated psychologists who believe that a solution to life's conflicts begins in a healthy orgasm. We have books that tell us all we need to know about sex, replacing the books that did the same for social etiquette. Even blatant descriptions of sex are said to be in the service of sublime, long-term relationships. More usually, they are used to achieve intense pleasure without worrying about long-term commitment. As a culture, our profound deficiency is in long-term interpersonal relationships.

Contemporary men and women seem afraid to experience long-term union with anything outside the self. This has value for maintaining psychological integrity, but it has the disadvantage of making one incapable of love. Existentialist philosophers have been profoundly aware of this problem in twentieth-century life. They see it as our central weakness. To quote Erich Fromm, "The deepest need of man . . . is the need to overcome his separateness, to leave the prison of his aloneness." [1]

Love, like other forms of ecstasy, is a union and therefore helps us overcome our isolation. If we are to be capable of love, we must break down the walls between ourselves and our fellow beings. We must relearn how to merge with an Other. Too often we assume that possessiveness is a negative trait, an infantile behavior that should be discarded in maturity. We assume that to become adult we must become independent. It is true that each of us must develop a sense of ourselves as a unique individual if we are to adjust to our modern, fragmented, mobile society. But it is also necessary that we find the courage to give up our separateness and merge with another in an intimate, possessive, dependent, and ecstatic relationship.

This book does not explain "how to do it." It explores the nature of ecstatic experience and the constraints of human relating in the hope of better understanding the phenomenon of love. The quest is toward discovering ways of renewal, moments of rebirth and of ongoing bliss which are the rewards of struggling to sustain a long-term dyadic relationship.

2

The Experience of Ecstasy

ECSTASY, like love, is a universal human potential. It is a subjective state which defies easy definition. Such words as "rapture," "transport," "bliss," and "frenzy" share in its meaning. Mystical traditions create new words to help believers understand and attain their ultimate religious experience. Our own culture is now saturated with special words which attempt to describe extraordinary personal experience—"high," "turned on," "spaced out," "freaked out," "in another world," "+ 2" —which reflect contemporary man's interest in exploring "inner space" and spiritual systems.

Ecstatic states are extraordinary but also quite ordinary. They are discontinuous with everyday experience, yet everyone has felt at least a faint echo of them. Like hunger and sex, ecstasy is part of our biological heritage and the experiential repertoire of our species. As a neurophysiological activity, it can be defined and studied. As a subjective phenomenon, it acquires meaning through the symbols and values of a given culture. It is not limited by intelligence or social class; and it is not exclusive to those with access to drugs or special training. It may be intentionally evoked or spontaneously achieved. Some people work all their lives for it; others live for years without caring and suddenly find themselves transformed by a single experience.

The word "ecstasy" has remained relatively free from jargon

and overuse. It is not yet equated with the profane "high" of drinking the "in" brand of beer or buying another car, nor is it necessarily associated with off-beat mysticism and the arcane. Ecstasy still alludes to moments in our life cycle as well as to mystic realms. It has been used to describe childbirth, orgasm, and moments in the creative process as well as religious visions and the state of grace. Furthermore, ecstasy is derived from roots with functional meaning. It is formed from the Greek *"ec,"* "out of," plus *"histani,"* "to cause to stand." The word "ecstasy" literally means a state of being outside of one's person.

Ecstasy is defined here as *the subjective experience of union or merger with something other than "I."* "I" is taken to mean that which is experienced inside one's personal boundaries, the core, continuous identity that provides an awareness of separateness from others. *Ecstatic consciousness is a state in which the sense of one's "I," one's personal boundary, is lost through merger with something or someone else.* In this state we do not experience a separate identity, but rather feel fused with an "Other" and in touch with elements of our identity which go beyond the "I." The word "self" here means the aspects of consciousness that lie beyond the "I."

This approach is psychological. Ecstasy is conceptualized as an internal mental process, even though outside factors may be critical to its development. Thus it is not transmitted by outside forces whether extraterrestrial or abstract. Rather it is a potential within human beings which, like speech and self-knowledge, expands within us as subjectivity and identity develop.

Nor is ecstasy simply a strong adjective for positive emotion. In fact, it is neither a positive nor a negative state, but occurs on a different level of consciousness altogether, one in which our psychological potential for merger has been evoked. Ecstasy is a so-called "altered state of consciousness," or it can also be identified with the term "transpersonal psychology."[1] "Transpersonal" denotes "beyond the personal" or "transcending the 'I.'" When such transcendence involves an experience of merger, whether with a personal object (a lover or a group) or an impersonal object (a deity or a cosmic consciousness), it falls into the realm of ecstasy.

In exploring altered states of consciousness, it is important to remember that the phrase is misleading, for it implies that there is one "unaltered" state of consciousness which is commonly shared by human beings. As William James has pointed out:

> Our normal waking consciousness, rational consciousness as we call it, is but one special type of consciousness, whilst all about it, parted from it by the filmiest of screens, there lie potential forms of consciousness entirely different. We may go through life without suspecting their existence; but apply the requisite stimulus, and at a touch they are there in all their completeness, definite types of mentality which probably somewhere have their field of application and adaptation. No account of the universe in its totality can be final which leaves these other forms of consciousness quite disregarded. How to regard them is the question—for they are so discontinuous with ordinary consciousness. Yet they may determine attitudes though they cannot furnish formulas, and open a region though they fail to give a map.[2]

It is hard to imagine an individual with only one state of consciousness. Electroencephalographic (EEG) techniques, though still in their infancy, suggest that even the traditional dichotomy between sleep and waking is oversimplified. Sleep is not homogeneous, but composed of at least two separate states which differ in numerous ways, including dreaming. Waking consciousness is even more variegated. The functioning mind has been described by Mircea Eliade as a "rushing stream of states of consciousness." He defines yoga, a discipline entirely devoted to distinguishing and controlling mental experience, as "the refusal to let oneself be carried along" by that stream.[3] Through years of hard work, the yogi learns to keep himself at a particular level of consciousness for long periods of time. The levels of consciousness that are attained, however, are hardly what James would have called "rational consciousness."

The yogi is unusual because he acknowledges other states of

consciousness as the goal of his discipline. Chemists, athletes, actors, clerks, and assembly-line workers all develop and sustain a particular level of consciousness at which they work most effectively, but in these cases the mental states are by-products, not the goal itself. An individual focusses on the designated task and finds that he accomplishes it best and most comfortably in a particular mental set. He becomes expert at attaining and sustaining an adaptive state of consciousness which goes unnoticed as he performs his task. Usually, a state of consciousness is the indirect product of an activity. Within ecstatic traditions, it becomes an explicit goal.

Ecstasy alludes to a state of consciousness in which the individual experiences his "soul" or "ego" or "spirit" standing outside his body or in merger with something else. This calls to mind trances, seizures, hysteria, the entire gamut of Dionysian rituals in which ordinary behavior is suspended. Plato describes Socrates in such a state in *The Symposium*:

> . . . another servant came in and reported that our friend Socrates had retired into the portico of the neighboring house. "There he is fixed," said he, "and when I call to him he will not stir."
>
> "How strange," said Agathon, "then you must call him again, and keep calling him."
>
> "Let him alone," said my informant. "He has a way of stopping anywhere and losing himself without any reason. I believe that he will soon appear; do not therefore disturb him." [4]

The assumption of all present is that Socrates' transports are positive. Agathon begs to "have the benefit of those thoughts which came into your mind in the portico, and are now in your possession; for I am certain that you would not have come away until you had found what you sought." Socrates does not reveal what went on in his mind during his trance. In *The Phaedrus* he speaks at length while in an "ecstasy," but admits that much of what he says under these circumstances is misleading. Although the Greeks prayed to a muse to inspire them, they did not necessarily accept such inspiration as infallible.

Plato was unusual in his capacity to blend the logician and the mystic in harmonious accord. Some cultures fear ecstatic experience and murder its practitioners or isolate them in asylums on the assumption they are dangerous. One society often misunderstands the ecstatic manifestations of another society. Thus a missionary arriving on an island in Melanesia for the first time discovered the natives sitting peacefully in a group, neither moving nor speaking, and concluded that they were unproductive. He was amazed when he learned that they had just destroyed all their worldly possessions and had been fasting for two days.

> They all sat motionless and not a word was uttered for the several minutes that I stayed there looking at them. It was enough to make anyone furious, to see them behaving in this idiotic manner! A whole group of strong, well-built natives, wearing new clean clothes and sitting in silence like stones or tree-trunks in the full afternoon, instead of working or attending to some job like reasonable beings. You would have said that they were ripe for a lunatic asylum.[5]

The natives were participating in a profound cargo-cult ritual, the most important event of their year. Deep in an ecstatic trance, they destroyed their goods as a demonstration of their faith in the approach of a new cosmic era in which the dead would come to life and paradise would be on earth. Enraptured, they awaited the arrival of this transformation. To the Westerner, their behavior was ridiculous. For if the Westerner's goal is material productivity, then his mentality must be pragmatic; but if an islander's goal is ecstatic rapture, then the pragmatics of the situation simply do not arise. The same situation is reflected in another way when we see a yogi doing his exercises and think, "But he is just sitting there doing nothing." But the stillness, the apparent lassitude of the cultist, is experienced as something valuable from within even though it may look meaningless or silly from without. The process can operate in reverse. Hamlet, for example, would not kill his uncle/stepfather Claudius at prayer for fear his soul would go directly to heaven. The audience knows that Claudius is in despair and not praying effectively. Prayer looks much the same whether it is experienced as despair, rapture, or boredom.

Religious writers in the Western world have generally believed that ecstasy can either be sanctifying or demonic. In the sixteenth century, St. Teresa of Avila was often afraid she was being deluded by her visions and would have preferred to be led to union with God by a more reliable path. A Church court debated the legitimacy of her visions, finding that they represented the Spirit of God rather than the Devil, and canonized her. In fact, most cultures in which ecstatic states are not forbidden have some kind of metaphysical system to explain them. For example, some believe in the transmigration of souls, others that the Holy Ghost or some other spirit form enters the body. The concept of ecstasy is less easily understood by members of cultures which seek to explain reality in materialistic or scientific terms. In our own society there is a split between the subculture of drugs and the occult and the more conservative world of operations research and finance.

Investigators of both psychedelic drugs and shamanistic religions use the term "ecstasy" much as it is used here. Two important books in this latter field, for example, are titled *Shamanism: Archaic Techniques of Ecstasy* and *Ecstatic Religions.* Mushroom specialist R. Gordon Wasson defines ecstasy in relation to its Greek origins as a "flight of the soul from the body" and concludes that it precisely fits what he calls the "bemushroomed" condition. Wasson has described himself as "the first to be invited to partake in the agape of the sacred mushroom" with an Amerindian tribe in 1953. His "trip" was specifically shaped by the methods and beliefs of his tribal shaman; and though its effect was profound and apparently not demonic, he wisely cautions:

But ecstasy is not fun. In our everyday existence we divide experience into good and bad, "fun" and pain. There is a third category, ecstasy, that for most of us hovers off stage, a stranger we never meet. The divine mushroom introduces ecstasy to us. Your very soul is seized and shaken until it tingles, until you fear that you will never recover your equilibrium. After all, who will choose to feel undiluted awe, or to float through that door yonder into the divine presence? The unknowing vulgar abuse the word, and we must recapture its full and portentous sense.[6]

Wasson's subjective evaluation of the ecstatic experience contrasts interestingly with the clinical definition in the *Psychiatric Dictionary*:

This term was formerly used to denote a clinical syndrome "in which a person presents opposite phases of mental action, some faculties being exalted and others depressed, sensations and locomotions being suspended . . ." [1892]

In present-day psychiatry, the term ecstasy is confined for the most part to trance-states in which religious ideation or similar ideas of dedication and complete surrender occupy almost the entire field of consciousness.[7]

Psychiatry has always been peripherally interested in ecstatic states, if only to learn how to differentiate them from the psychotic process. Psychiatrists currently function as gatekeepers for society by defining insanity for the major culture much as earlier "experts," boards of priests, decided on which mystical visions were products of the Devil and which a sign of God's grace. There are many mental-health practitioners today who still consider mystical experiences as "delusions to be untangled."[8] The recent popularity of psychedelic drugs has increased the confusion between mysticism and madness. Drug states have been called "psychomimetic," implying that they provide the "model" for a psychotic episode. On the other hand LSD has been used as a therapeutic agent in schizophrenia and neurosis.

Increasing numbers of psychiatrists, influenced by Jung's concepts of archetypes and the collective unconscious, have studied psychotic experience as if it were analogous to or even another form of mystical experience. For example, John Perry finds a progression of themes in individual psychotic episodes which are similar to archetypal progression in man, cultural myths, and mystic vision.[9] This kind of thinking has inspired treatment settings (for appropriate patients) in which psychosis is viewed as a journey into the self. The therapist's job is redefined so that he may function as an interpreter and guide to the trip, much as gurus and spiritual teachers guide the mystical journeys of their seekers. R. D. Laing's work with schizophrenic patients also emphasizes the growth potential of a descent into one's own insanity as a reality which may contain essential truths for the individual's perception of himself and the world around him.

Perhaps the most important outcome of psychiatry's role conflict between administrator and guide has been the enormous increase in interest in other states of consciousness as a legitimate field for research and study. Psychiatrists and psychologists are trained in accepting other states of consciousness as real and relevant factors in human behavior. Delusions and hallucinations dominate many of their patients' worlds. Intense psychotherapy with relatively healthy patients almost always uncovers subjective phenomena which go beyond commonplace assumptions about mental processes. Recently, psychological theorists have turned their attention to ecstasy as an aspect of normal human experience rather than as a sign of mental malfunction. They are investigating the positive, non-pathological aspects of altered states of consciousness.

Abraham Maslow has studied what he terms "peak-experience" from this point of view. Maslow found that there was a general inadequacy of words or concepts with which to communicate with others about peak-experiences. Many people he interviewed did not seem to know what he was talking about. At first he divided the world into "peakers" and "non-peakers." Then he discovered that if he pursued the conversation with someone who seemed to be a non-peaker, and if the discussion were supplemented with examples and gestures, he would usually find that the apparent non-peaker did have some glimmer of peak-experience in his life. This led Maslow to believe that every human being is capable of peaking, although some people inhibit the experience:

I finally began to use the word "non-peaker" to describe not the person who is unable to have peak-experiences, but rather the person who is afraid of them, who suppresses them, who denies them, who turns away from them, or who "forgets" them.[10]

There are probably many reasons why people hold themselves back from peak-experiences. Maslow found that certain kinds of personalities were more likely to be non-peakers than others.

Any person whose character structure . . . forces him to try to be extremely or completely rational or "materialistic" or mechanistic tends to become a non-peaker. That is, such a view of life tends to make the person regard his peak and transcendent experiences as a kind of insanity, a complete loss of control, a sense of being overwhelmed by irrational emotion, etc. The person who is afraid of going insane and who is, therefore, desperately hanging on to stability, control, reality, etc., seems to be frightened by peak-experiences and tends to fight them off. For the compulsive-obsessive person, who organizes his life around the denying and controlling emotions, the fear of being overwhelmed by an emotion (which is interpreted as a loss of control) is enough for him to mobilize all his stamping-out and defensive activities against the peak-experience. I have one instance of a very convinced Marxian who denied—that is, who turned away from—a legitimate peak-experience, finally classifying it as some kind of peculiar but unimportant thing that had happened but that had best be forgotten because this experience conflicted with her whole materialistic mechanistic philosophy of life. I have found a few non-peakers who were ultra-scientific, that is, who espoused the nineteenth century conception of science as an unemotional or anti-emotional activity which was ruled entirely by logic and rationality and who thought anything which was not logical and rational had no respectable place in life. (I suspect also that extremely "practical" i.e. . . . exclusively means-oriented, people will turn out to be non-peakers, since such experiences earn no money, bake no bread, and chop no wood.) So also for extremely other-directed people, who scarcely know what is going on inside themselves.[11]

Maslow's understanding of ecstatic experience from a psychological perspective has helped to disentangle peak-experience from psychopathology. He sought out the healthiest and most creative individuals for subjects and found that those who did not have peak-experiences were the exceptions. By showing that peak-experience was a normal human phenomenon, he shifted the focus of interest toward questioning the nature of the experience itself rather than its relationship to insanity or isolated cultish practice.

Ours being a scientific and technological age, it is no surprise that even in this highly experiential area, research has focussed mostly on understanding multiple techniques for altering states of consciousness rather than on the nature of the experience. Of course, we have learned a great deal through such an approach, and in particular we know that many common mental mechanisms are involved in disparate forms of ecstatic experience. Moreover, anthropological evidence suggests that ecstatic traditions, no matter how geographically and temporally diverse, share the same technology for achieving ecstasy. Systems may vary and the number and status of individuals who devote their lives to ecstasy often change. But at the heart of the matter are a few basic techniques—most of which have also been explored by individuals who have neither name nor system for what they are doing.

The ecstatic experience is interpreted differently by the various sects, tribal rituals, and mass religious movements; but at its height, the goal of the experience is always the loss of "I," merger, the sensation of oneness and unity. It consists of a continuum of states in which the individual experiences himself to be in touch with things that are usually outside his "I." The peaking individual may be working so creatively with an artistic medium (paint, stone, words) that his consciousness becomes identical with the form itself. He may be making love, caressing another body that seems to be an extension of himself and yet acts and reacts in far more subtle and unpredictable ways. He may be beating on a drum or dancing rhythmically with a large group, gradually increasing the pace until he is conscious of nothing but movement toward catharsis. He may also be in a mystical rapture in which he experiences a blinding vision of ultimate reality.

The experience of ecstatic merger has been described by many people and in many different ways. D. H. Lawrence has described two men wrestling as a struggle toward rapturous union: "They seemed to drive their white flesh deeper and deeper against each other, as if they would break into oneness." [12] Similarly, in sexual ecstasy, union may be described as moving beyond the joining of bodies toward a total fusion. In Tantra Yoga, "the inexpressible experience of unity" which results from ritual intercourse

> is called samarasa . . . ; that is, a state which is nirvanic. Time and eternity become one, Shiva and Shakti are wed within the sadhaka's own being and he knows the totalization that preceded creation of the universe.[13]

With drugs the essential experience can be the same. Stanislav Grof thus describes his experience with LSD under stroboscopic lights:

> . . . a very powerful experience of cosmic unity—a feeling that I was leaving my body and expanding to cosmic proportions. The memory of this experience of mystic oneness with what there is has stayed with me ever since.[14]

This experience was particularly sought by the transcendentalists of the nineteenth century. Walt Whitman described the poet's consciousness in this way:

I celebrate myself, and sing myself,
And what I assume you shall assume,
For every atom belonging to me as good belongs
to you.
. . .
In all people I see myself, none more and not one
barleycorn less.

. . .
To me the converging objects of the universe
perpetually flow,
All are written to me, and I must get what
*the writing means.**

Religious mystics have also spent much time trying to give us an idea of what they have experienced; for example:

What I want to explain is the soul's feelings when it is in this divine union. It is plain enough what union is; in union two separate things become one. . . . The will must be fully occupied in loving, but does not understand how it loves.[15]

If we are to experience merger, our ordinary frame of reality (which assumes that we are separate from one another and the world around us) must be dissipated. When the "I" dissolves, the within and without coalesce and "reality" changes. We enter the world of fantasies, dreams, myths, archetypes, illusions, and hallucinations which come from levels of "self" devoid of the organizing functions of the "I." What we see and feel take on different meanings. The thought processes of someone on LSD, in profound meditation, or during orgasm reflect these new perceptions.

Ecstatic journeys tend to follow a certain order, as if the brain has only a few stereotyped paths with which to order an "I-less" world. The experience of merger is a sweeping transformation of our ordinary frame of reality. As the organizing "I" is weakened, the "self" defines another reality which lies between the subjective awareness of separateness and merger. This new realm has an order which ordinary perception may not encompass; and this order is defined by the common denominator in the allegorical stories of childhood, adult fantasies, and occult religious tracts. Sometimes the path is described in coded or numerological

* From "Song of Myself," from *Leaves of Grass,* by Walt Whitman. Published by Doubleday & Company, Inc.

fashion, as in alchemy, or through a historico-religious system like the *Divine Comedy*. Sometimes the Way is seen through analogy with the order of the universe, as in astrology, or with the structure of the human body, as in the Sefiroth of the Kabbala or in Kundalini Yoga. In each case, the meaning is taken to be mystically more than the matter. When Jesus said: "Take this bread to be my body, and this wine to be my blood," he transformed the reality of the bread and that of his body into a cosmic metaphor in which the secular act of eating becomes an ecstatic partaking of God. In the profound myths of an ecstatic Way, the symbols stand both in their literal and cosmic contexts as they appeal to the self-conscious "I" and lead to the transformed levels of understanding of the states of "self."

Each ecstatic tradition tries to guide its adherents along their own path in stages (trials, temptations, levels) until the final goal of merger (nirvana, the clear light, samhadi) is achieved. The stages may amount to a lifetime path which is rarely traversed successfully (such as that long struggle represented by Bunyan in *Pilgrim's Progress*). The Way is easily lost and the order obfuscated through temporal and political attrition. It may become the foundation for a myth of hidden secrets, buried treasures, or lost continents, all of which are common in occult writing. Few learn to experience the ecstatic meaning of the myth. It is perpetuated on its secular level, taken as concrete reality, or by the more sophisticated as being a good logical discipline or of historical interest.

During initial "enlightenment," the instant ecstasies of trance-like conversions and drug trips, these stages may be telescoped into minutes. Acute experiences usually begin with the *primary merger state* and progress through a *period of visions and archetypal fantasies* to the final *re-entry phase* in which perceptions and meaning are experienced as heightened but converging on a continuum with non-ecstatic reality. In the case of a drug where the duration of the effect is relatively constant, this tripartite progression is predictable on an almost hour-to-hour basis. In ecstatic states such as those induced by prolonged meditation, the time course depends on the individual's concentration and the power of the method. Even so, an experienced guide can follow the pattern of the journey and thereby help with difficult transitions.

To follow the route of an ecstatic journey the traveler should be familiar with its tradition and symbols. Individuals with a common tradition can more easily recognize the movement of the experience. Although the most profound merger states transcend all verbal forms, the middle state between merger and the return of the "I" in the re-entry phase is definitely shaped by cultural expectations. Tibetan monks experience a set of deities different from that of Christian mystics or followers of the Kabbala. And yet, as Jung and many other students of the experience have pointed out, the threads that unite the various visionary systems are far more striking than the differences.

Timothy Leary borrowed *The Tibetan Book of the Dead*, the *Bardo Thodol*, as a meaningful guide for his followers in their own psychedelic experiences.[16] The *Bardo Thodol* was recited to shape the death trip of certain Tibetan Buddhist monks. Leary's manual is divided into three states or bardos. The First Bardo, akin to the initial state of merger, is described as a period of "primary, clear light," of "ego loss." The second is the Period of Hallucinations and is peopled by heroic personages which inhabit the world of Buddhist teachings. The visions take the form of polarities (between the sexes, good and evil, light and dark); of miraculous voyages and adventures; and of heroes, sages, magicians, and archetypal families. Leary translates some of the Buddhist detail into the more Western imagery of Hesse's "magic theater" and pseudo-scientific molecular jargon. The Third Bardo narrates the re-entry phase in terms of the illusions about supernatural powers and the ego traps that may result from mistaking the mental boundary of the magical mind with the "reality" boundary of the unmagical world. For Leary this is the mechanism of the "bad trip," the suicidal seven-story plunge of the acidhead who mistakes mental "flying" for supernatural abilities.

The stereotypical nature of ecstatic experience is *not* a limitation upon the potential profundity of an individual's quest any more than the body's limited number of neurological reflexes diminishes the beauty and intricacy of the nervous system. Rather it is a statement about the underlying similarity in all human functioning at the essential levels. On a physiological level the brain, like all organs, has only a few common pathways which can be activated in the face of a wide variety of stimulation. Cultural learning and individual experience may shape the content of our thought patterns but the form of cerebral output, like the motor-reflex arc determined by the attachment of muscles, is tethered to our anatomy even in the most sublime experience.

The common elements in ecstatic consciousness are demonstrated in the stereotyped ways in which these states may be induced. Induction techniques are mechanisms that support the dissolution of the "I" and the entrance into other states of consciousness, including ecstatic merger states. Most of these techniques alter the sense of "I" by radically shifting the usual input of information to the brain. That is, they change the nature of the ordinary reality which the "I" perceives and which supports its boundary functions. Sitting absolutely still for many hours in meditation, whirling dervish-like in a dance, or taking a psychedelic drug may all result in blazing union with a transcendent reality. What they have in common is a forced shift in some patterns of sensation which usually are routinely processed. Apparently, once the ordinary sensory input (from within and without) shifts, the potential for other states of consciousness, including ecstasy, shifts as well.

Research into sensory deprivation provides some rich examples of this mechanism. Initial medical interest in deprivation occurred during a polio epidemic in Boston when patients were placed in great iron-lung machines and the overburdened nursing staff had little time to attend to their social needs. These conditions deprived the patients of normal intensity and variation of sensory input. Many reported strange mental phenomena which included hearing voices and seeing visions. At first, medical personnel thought the patients had contracted a new variety of polio which affected cerebral as well as peripheral functioning. But they discovered that a radio or frequent nursing contacts reduced the intensity of bizarre mental phenomena. In fact, the conditions of sensory deprivation within the iron-lung machines, not the polio virus, were the responsible factor.

Thus we respond to the sudden *absence* of a stimulus that has passed unnoticed in its continuous presence. We all know what it feels like to remove a hat that we have been wearing for a long time. We experience a ghost-hat, a sense of pressure along the point of circumference where the hat made contact with our head. We had become habituated to the hat while it was on and unmindful of its pressure, but soon after removing it we find ourselves tentatively patting our heads to reassure ourselves that we in fact took it off. Or living near a freeway we get used to the steady drone of traffic. If, in the dead of night, there is a period when no cars or trucks go by, we may wake up, startled by the unexpected silence. In situations of more extreme sensory deprivation, all the senses may haunt us until we hallucinate visions, sounds, and touch, even smells and tastes. Any change in normal conditions of stimulus forces a heightened perception of sensations, ideas, and emotions which are usually ignored as a part of ourselves unrelated to our "anticipated environment." These changes can be interpreted as either psychopathological or part of our positive psychological potential.

Experiments in sensory deprivation also have provided a clue to certain kinds of psychotic manifestations that previously had been a mystery. A small but constant percentage of patients coming out of open-heart surgery tend to hallucinate. So do patients on kidney machines. Military personnel who watch radar screens for eight hours continuously have recounted similar experiences. A shift in the sensory environment, most easily provided by human contact, puts an end to the phenomena. Most investigators interpret the condition as pathological. Delgado thus describes the experience of his subjects:

some . . . reported sensations of movement or touch, of feelings of "otherness," or that another body was lying beside them on the bed. Isolation also tended to increase the belief in supernatural phenomena and several of the students reported that for a few days after their isolation experiment, they were afraid that they were going to see ghosts.[17]

Delgado and his associates concluded that human beings need a changing sensory environment. Under deprivation conditions, in their opinion, the brain ceases to function in an adequate—that is, normal—way.

But supposing these shifts from normal states of consciousness are *not* viewed as frightening or pathological, but simply as an experiential threshold to another state of awareness which has meaning beyond the ordinary? John Lilly immersed himself in 93° water for indefinite periods to test the theory that the brain needs external stimulation to stay awake. He discovered entirely unexpected phenomena:

In the absence of all stimulation it was found that one quickly makes up for this by an extremely heightened awareness and increasing sensory experience in the absence of known means of external stimulation. Within the first few hours it was found that I did not tend to go to sleep at all. The original theory was wrong. One did not need external stimulation to stay awake. After a few tens of hours of experiences, I found phenomena that had been previously described in various literatures. I went through dreamlike states, trancelike states, mystical states. In all these states, I was totally intact, centered, and there. At no time did I lose conscious awareness of the facts of the experiment. Some part of me always knew that I was suspended in water in a tank in the dark and in the silence.

I went through experiences in which other people apparently joined me in this dark silent environment. I could actually see them, feel them, and hear them. At other times, I went through dreamlike sequences, waking dreams as they are now called, in which I watched what was happening. At other times I apparently tuned in on networks of communication that are normally below our levels of awareness, networks of civilizations way beyond ours. I did hours of work on my own hindrances to understanding myself, or my life situation. I did hours of meditation, concentration, and contemplation, without knowing that this was what I was doing. It was only later in reading the literature that I found that the states that I was getting into resembled those attained by other techniques.[18]

There is no factual discrepancy between Lilly's descriptions and Delgado's of his students. However, there is a marked difference in the context of the experiences. The student experiments were done in a clinical setting with little validation of their new subjectivity except as pathological phenomena.[19] Lilly performed his experiments outside the clinical framework. He seems to have been personally ready to view altered mental states from a more positive perspective.

There are other ways to change sensory input that will affect states of consciousness. Sensory overload, for example, has much the same effect as sensory deprivation. Pounding music and stroboscopic lights produce radical changes in mental functioning. Tribal rituals also use sensory overload in the form of frantic music and dancing to induce trance states. But ecstatic consciousness is the product not only of altered sensory input. For ecstatic experience to develop there must be a powerful context and ideological system to support altered consciousness. Changing the sensory input is one frequently used means to transcend ordinary reality and the state of consciousness that is its mirror; but without a system, such a change has no meaning.

The discovery by Olds and Milner of a so-called "pleasure center" in the vicinity of the septal area of the midbrain of mammals suggests even more direct access to changes of consciousness in the near future. Animals who are wired to press a lever and stimulate themselves in this area prefer its effects to food and sex. They are even willing to sustain severe punishment in order to repeat the stimulation. For ethical reasons, experiments in similar stimulation of humans have been limited, but the few accounts available (in patients with severe neurological illnesses) suggest a powerful positive experience which is often interpreted in sexual terms by both the patient and the physician. The following reaction took place in a patient with septal electrode implants:

> The patient's narcolepsy was severe. He would move from an alert state into a deep sleep in the matter of a second. Recognizing that button pressing promptly awakened him, fellow patients and friends occasionally resorted to pushing the button if he fell asleep so rapidly that he was unable to stimulate himself.
>
> The patient, in explaining why he pressed the septal button with such frequency, stated that the feeling was "good;" it was as if he were building up to a sexual orgasm. He reported that he was unable to achieve the orgastic end point, however, explaining that his frequent, sometimes frantic, pushing of the button was an attempt to reach the end point. This futile effort was frustrating at times and described by him on these occasions as a "nervous feeling." [20]

Heath describes another patient with intracranial electrodes in place:

> Actual content varied considerably, but regardless of his baseline emotional state and the subject under discussion in the room, the stimulation was accompanied by the patient's introduction of a sexual subject, usually with a broad grin. When questioned about this, he would say, "I don't know why that came to mind—I just happened to think of it." The "happy feelings" with mesencephalic stimulation were not accompanied by sexual thought.[21]

Recent work has linked the smoking of marijuana to electrical activity in the septal area as recorded from intracranial electrodes:

> Numerous previous reports have indicated the relationship of feelings of euphoria and well-being with high amplitude slow wave activity in the septal region. The present patient reported feelings of euphoria while smoking marijuana, coincident with the appearance of high amplitude slow wave activity from the implanted electrodes in the septal region. Previous reports have documented no significant change from conventional scalp EEG's in men using marijuana.[22]

Like research into sensory deprivation, one fascinating aspect of the above neurophysiological findings on pleasure (and perhaps ecstasy) is the power of context on the subject's report. In Delgado's clinical reports in *The Physical Control of the Mind*, the importance of the dyadic context and sex is striking. The patients were aware of their implants and knew that the doctor had control over the stimulation. The sensations were therefore experienced as something he was "doing" to them (a literal case of "you turn me on"). An eleven-year-old boy frankly acknowledged the pleasure he experienced during stimulation of an area located on the surface of the left temporal lobe, commenting: "Hey! You can keep me here longer when you give me these; I like those." When this area was stimulated, he also indicated his fondness for the male interviewer, introduced the subject of sex play, and showed considerable sexual confusion (was he a boy or a girl?), implying that he would like to be a girl and marry the interviewer.[23]

Two female patients in their thirties both responded to similar stimulation by making romantic overtures to the male therapist. They reported enjoying a pleasant tingling sensation and became unusually talkative and overtly flirtatious. The interpretation of the sensation as sexual/romantic is presumably related to the one-to-one interpersonal situation. A patient with an implantation that caused him frequently to bend over always found an explanation for his unpredictable behavior. If he were in an office he would say that he was searching for a book; in a bedroom, he said he was looking for a slipper. His interpretation of his movements was adapted to his environment. Perhaps those patients who interpreted their septal stimulation as sexual might have viewed the same experience otherwise in a different environment. Similarly, the therapist or guide and the setting are critically important to the sensations, imagery, and interpretation of a psychedelic drug experience. Thus it is no new or startling finding that context is a relevant variable in determining behavior. In fact, during the induction of ecstasy, context is far more than a background environmental influence. It is in many ways *the* beginning experience for the individual.

Ecstasy is a merger experience which transcends the "I," which is beyond boundaries and differences. The ultimate experience of union is variously labeled as the unmade, the unborn, the void, "the nervous system devoid of mental-conceptual activity." [24] All these are phrases which imply the total absence of distinctions between self and other. But the induction of an ecstatic state begins in an already formed environment. The environment is a template in the movement toward merger, whether with a concrete or an abstract object. There are critical differences within individuals and among traditions in the choice of ecstatic routes and in assumptions about object and fusion. These differences are reflected in the choice of environment and techniques of induction as well as in the interpretation of the experience.

Some ecstatic journeys are begun in *isolation* from others. The dissolution of "I" is facilitated by an impersonal object used to focus concentration. Some are begun in the presence of an "Other." The dissolution of "I" is facilitated by *dyadic merger,* by the bonding of love. Others are begun in the company of many others. The dissolution of the "I" is facilitated by *merger with the group.* Some individuals begin ecstatic journeys in all these ways and others find all doors closed to them. But most of us prefer one or another ecstatic route; that is, we develop an *ecstatic orientation* which guides our ecstatic preferences much as sexual orientation guides our sexual preferences.

The various traditions that support ecstatic experience mirror these three basic orientations. In some traditions monks take vows of silence or solitude and seek isolation as a route toward merger with totality. Others support dyadic merger as the Sacred Way by providing a guide, partner, or semi-divine leader. Still others use the presence of a large congregation for a group experience. The merger experience at the core of all ecstasy transcends these differences in orientation. The boundary between solitary, dyadic, and group orientations is not fixed and unyielding. Nevertheless, the chosen orientation does affect the nature of the ecstatic experience and helps define the characteristics of the tradition. Ecstatic orientations are firmly rooted in the development of ecstatic consciousness and are the guides and signposts for religions and societies. They spell out the Way in which ecstasy is to be pursued.

That orientation which makes use of solitude and isolation to achieve ecstatic experience is most highly developed in special orders of religious traditions which also resort to prayer, meditation, and contemplation. In general, members of these groups, no matter what their formal system of belief, withdraw from the complicated stimulations of the everyday world and adopt the life style of hermits and monks. They model themselves after the psalmist's verse: "I would get me away, far off, and remain in solitude." Worldly isolation often includes extreme forms of sensory deprivation. A disciplined mystic learns how to sit motionless for hours, fast for days, remain celibate for years, restricting all external change to an absolute minimum. The goal is to free the mind and body from trivial habits so that other levels of consciousness, including the ecstatic, may be released and experienced. Farid al-din 'Attar, a saint and mystic, instructs the Sufi on how to achieve the desired state:

> Clothe thyself with the garment of nothingness and drink the cup of annihilation. Cover thy breast with a nothingness and draw over thy head the robe of non-existence. Set thy foot in the stirrup of complete renunciation and, looking straight before thee, ride the steed of non-being to the place where nothing is.[25]

"The place where nothing is" has been experienced variously as the cloud of unknowing, the dark night of the soul, the void, the state of instructed unknowing; it is a stage that has a place in all of the mystical traditions but is described in different terms by each. Even scientific non-religious, humanistic psychology has had something to say about this state of consciousness:

Psychologically, continuous repetition of the same stimulus may be considered the equivalent of no stimulation at all. The two situations, which from the psychological and physiological points of view are quite similar, insofar as they restrict awareness to that of a single source of unchanging stimulation, also seem to produce the same effects. So we can say (within our frame of reference) that concentrative meditation is a practical technique which uses an experiential knowledge of the structure of our nervous system to "turn off" awareness of the external world and produce a state of blank-out or darkness, the "void," the cloud of unknowing. The techniques of concentrative meditation are not deliberately mysterious or exotic but are simply a matter of practical applied psychology.[26]

Any of the senses can be used as a take-off point to get beyond the senses. Any stimulation provided at regular intervals at a constant level of intensity causes neurological habituation; that is, the nervous system stops interpreting the information. For example, in experiments in which the image presented to the retina of the eye is stabilized, it was found that the image tends to disappear completely. The subject reports that he has blanked out, that he is not seeing. For the eye as for other sensory organs, stimulation at a regular frequency and at constant intensity habituates the brain; the electroencephalogram measuring electrical activity of the brain is just as reactive. Continuation of stimulation at constant intensity and regular frequency has the same effect as sensory deprivation; the brain receives no differential messages from the sense organs, no support of an "I" based on changing external realities.

Mystical practice has preceded, of course, scientific explanation. As if to take advantage of the deprivation effect of continuous stimulus, religions often present the worshipper with a single external object which helps him to focus his concentration on one particular sense. It can be visual, as with a mandala, a flame, or an icon; aural, as with a mantra or a koan; tactile or kinesthetic, as in dervish twirling or the steady movement of a hand drawing a circle over and over and over; or gustatory and olfactory, as with incense, oil, or a drop of wine. The most effective objects suggest to the worshipper the nature of the reality for which he strives. Thus mandalas are traditionally simple, abstract, balanced, and centered, like samadhi. Icons, in contrast, represent a compassionate or suffering figure. Objects of meditation are generally ambiguous and reflect an order that matches the metaphysic of the culture making use of them. Many people no doubt would be turned off by the mantra that scientist-physician John Lilly found particularly effective:

> I am not the biocomputer. I am not the programmer.
> I am not the programming. I am not the programmed.
> I am not the program.[27]

Lilly's mantra shows that although the repetition of a stimulus is a critical factor in the induction of ecstatic states, the content is not irrelevant. A specific sensory mode may be effective for some but be non-viable to others. A specific content which triggers an exotic sensuality, childhood reverie, or religious belief may be an important factor in facilitating induction.

The object of meditation may be devoid of all mystical or God-directed relevance as long as it and the situation do not actually bias the subject against altering his state of consciousness. For example, Arthur Deikman conducted research on the effects of meditation by asking his subjects to concentrate on a blue vase in an otherwise plain and rather empty room during half-hour sessions over a period of several months. The subjects were told to try to "see the vase as it exists in itself, without any connection to other things. Exclude all other thoughts or feelings or sounds or body sensations . . . Let the perception of the vase fill your entire mind." The subjects were all untrained in traditional techniques of meditation and yet they rapidly began to experience changes in the vase and in themselves. They noted increased vividness and animation; some even experienced a sense of merger or fusion with the vase. "When the vase changes shape, I feel this in my body."[28]

Experimental data on EEG responses of yogis during and after meditation shed some light on this effect.

During the meditation and during the withdrawal there was no response in the yogi's brain to external stimuli. When the yogi was not meditating, repetition of the external stimulus showed no habituation, as it presumably would have occurred in other subjects.[29]

In other words, by learning to be so totally non-reactive to his environment, the yogi can subsequently experience that same environment more acutely. He can maintain an awareness of the steady tick of a clock without tuning it out. He is able to let his entire sensory in-put flow through his nervous system, transcending the usual selective inhibitions of the brain:

Those who flow as life flows know
They need no other force:
They feel no wear, they feel no tear,
They need no mending, no repair.[30]

Even temporary experience of concentration on an object may produce a startling freshness when the individual resumes normal sensory input. Some of us have idiosyncratic techniques to experience our work and home anew. We go for a walk, stand in the shower, swim, enjoy a steam bath, play tennis, or take a nap in order to blank out the specific work tasks to which our minds have become dulled. Many artists and theorists use these techniques to stimulate their creativity.

Most of us are able to attain more or less ecstatic levels of consciousness if we can effectively concentrate on a gratifying sensual object. We can become absorbed in Beethoven's Ninth, Picasso's *Guernica*, Yeats's *Leda and the Swan*; repetitive tasks like pottery making, carpentry, or rhythmic sports can catch us up in a special moment of subjectivity different from and more intense than what is usual. Tennyson developed a personal system from his mundane environment:

A kind of waking trance—this for lack of a better word—I have frequently had, quite up from boyhood, when I have been all alone. This has come upon me through repeating my own name to myself silently, till all at once, as it were out of the intensity of the consciousness of individuality, individuality itself seemed to dissolve and fade away into boundless being, and this not a confused state but the clearest, the surest of the surest, utterly beyond words—where death was an almost laughable impossibility—the loss of personality (if so it were) seeming no extinction, but the only true life. I am ashamed of my feeble description. Have I not said the state is utterly beyond words? [31]

Such experiences are rarely thought of as ecstatic—only pleasurable changes from day-to-day events, from day-to-day consciousness. Tennyson is an unusual extreme. Usually, we focus on an activity which produces an interruption in routine consciousness (tennis, pottery, music) rather than on the mental state itself, for it is this focus which functions in place of an object of meditation to induce a change of consciousness. These experiences are gentle ventures into the ecstatic world. Frequently, part of the "I" is held back; part of consciousness continues to work on the problems of the day.

Ecstatic states that are tied to a more purposeful and disciplined use of these techniques break the knot with the world of affairs. The seeker must enter the other consciousness, accept the visions, hallucinations, and mythic projections as pathways to final merger states. Religious disciplines strive to train the mind to shape the chaos and fear of altered mental functioning into new and meaningful patterns which reflect a larger metaphysic.

Because the experience literally transforms consciousness, a creative person may attempt to change the world he lives in to support his visions. Paul's singular experience of enlightenment on the road to Damascus and his subsequent organizational fervor reflect such an effort. Some mystics, like William Blake, develop a personal theology. Blake felt that in order for a system of belief to be intense and profoundly meaningful, it had to be his own. He attempted to make every moment alive with ecstatic meaning.

The essence of the ecstatic orientation of solitude is to eschew another individual or group. Other people are often perceived as demonic temptors. The responsibilities of being in the world become distractions. An ecstatic orientation which emphasizes social isolation and techniques of deprivation is dependent on a culture which allows such blatant disengagement from the demands and responsibilities of ordinary worldly cycles. In our society, this orientation is a deviation from social requirements. Even priests are expected to form "relevant" relationships. In addition, the politics of a sect that teaches concentrated meditation may themselves become entanglements that prevent total dedication to attaining ecstatic states. Hindu society evolved a system for protecting mystics and creating a place for them to achieve their special states. Once a holy man has proved his value and worked to a degree that he can achieve extraordinary feats of meditation, he earns the right to a temple, a sponsor, and helpers who make sure that he is not interrupted while in a special state of consciousness.

Systems of belief which emphasize the abstract or impersonal nature of ultimate union are most fully representative of the solitary ecstatic orientation. In most Oriental religious and mystic philosophies, the final breakthrough is described as mysterious and ineffable; it is not attributed to the intervention of a spirit or deity from another realm of being. When deities appear, they are generally thought of as facilitating agents in the sense that by concentrating on their attributes, the devout person can more speedily attain the state he is seeking. According to Swami Satchidananda:

> And that one has no name, no form, no place . . . But such abstractions cannot be grasped by our limited minds . . . that is why, according to our capacity, the Infinite One reduces himself to a lower level.[32]

In a sense, deities are transitional objects. A security blanket helps a child adapt to the transition between being in his mother's arms and being on his own. A deity represents a transitional stage between relating to an abstraction and relating to a mortal person. Usually, the worship of God (or one of many gods) manifests a solitary ecstatic orientation, but it often assumes forms which are close to a dyadic orientation as the worshipper experiences a real interactive relationship with the divine Other.

The attributes of deities can be used as objects of contemplation. Plato believed that images and holy statuary stimulated a memory of "true being." Any object of beauty in the real world, particularly human, reflected the greater reality that had been known before birth:

> Every soul of man has in the way of nature beheld true being; this was the condition of her passing into the form of man . . . Few only retain an adequate remembrance of them; and they, when they behold here any image of that other world, are rapt in amazement; but they are ignorant of what this rapture means, because they do not clearly perceive . . . they are seen through a glass dimly; and there are few who, going to the images, behold in them the realities, and these only with difficulty.[33]

Plato describes Socrates as a true philosopher, one who seeks knowledge of the absolutes which lie behind material images. His is just one of a myriad of explanations of why contemplation of an object or a person can lead to an ecstatic sense of awe, but the experience itself seems universal.

Both Judaism and Christianity include a non-personal mysticism as well as one oriented toward a personal deity. For most worshippers the personages of Jehovah and particularly of Jesus are less routes to an abstract totality than to Totality itself. Christian mysticism often seems closer to the dyadic mode than the solitary; merger with God is commonly described in the language of human love and often becomes intensely sexual. The ultimate goal is still the dissolution of the "I" and merger, yet the form is personal and intimate.

St. Teresa of Avila is an articulate Christian mystic who has delineated the steps of progressively intense and profound ecstatic union with God. Her central allegory is reflected in the title of her book, *The Interior Castle.* The door to the castle, she maintains, is prayer. In prayer, the soul enters into itself and progresses from mansion to mansion, toward increasingly intense inner life. In meditation, a beginning devout may have to rely on such mental tricks as repeating the words of a simple, well-known prayer and considering their meanings or concentrating on visual images of the life of Christ.

Teresa describes the progressive techniques that the worshipper can use after he learns to focus his mind in prayer. Through active recollection he can achieve "the Prayer of Quiet," a state in which the external body is as asleep but the memory alert and awake. Teresa's theology attributes this state and the ultimate stage, "the Prayer of Union," to the intervention of God, who actively enters the soul of the devout. She was aware of various kinds of ecstasy, including raptures (in which the soul dissolves outward rather than soaring upward), flights of the soul, visions, internal conversations, and, ultimately, ecstatic pain. In general, the more violent ecstasies were brief, but a full sense of union could go on for days. She attempts to describe the state:

> While seeking God in this way, the soul is conscious that it is fainting almost completely away in a kind of swoon, with a very great calm and joy. Its breath and all its bodily powers progressively fail it, so that it can hardly stir its hands without great effort. Its eyes close involuntarily, but if they remain open, they see almost nothing. . . . He hears but does not understand what he hears. In the same way, his senses serve no purpose except to do him harm. It is the same with the tongue, for he cannot form a word, nor would he have the strength to pronounce one. The whole physical strength vanishes and the strength of the soul increases for the better enjoyment of its bliss. . . .
>
> I was wondering when I decided to write this—after taking Communion and experiencing that state of prayer of which I am writing—how the soul is occupied at that time. The Lord said to me: "It dissolves utterly, my daughter, to rest more and more in Me. It is no longer itself that lives; it is I." As it cannot comprehend what it understands, it understands by not understanding.[34]

God's concerned, paternal relationship was as real to St. Teresa as any interaction in her life.

The second ecstatic orientation, that of the dyad, is less generally acknowledged as a Way than mystical union with a deity or with an abstract Absolute. True dyadic merger consists in two people forming a union in which both actively work toward dissolution of the "I" in or with the Other. Dyadic ecstasy is love—ecstasy in the context of an interpersonal relationship.

St. Teresa (and many other mystics following a solitary Way) experienced union with a personal God and described that union as Love. There is no clear line between paths that use a divine Other and those which use a mortal. Worship of saints and deities in pantheons is a clear use of the human qualities of immortals to facilitate an experience of trust and union in the worshipper. Many cultures cherish myths of individuals who achieve immortal bliss through union with a deity. Zeus's sexual contact with mortals provided temporary ecstasy for his partners and resulted in semi-divine children. Jesus, similarly, is important simultaneously for his mortal suffering and for his divine attributes.

It is not unusual for a mortal to be taken as a god. The rulers of ancient Rome and Egypt were routinely worshipped. Sub-groups of our own culture occasionally deify their leader, as the examples of Father Divine and Maharaj-ji show in this century. When not actually deified, a strong charismatic leader often functions in a quasi-religious way as priest or shaman. He may be the focus of a group, but each member experiences his union as with the individual leader rather than with the group as a whole. Thus the legends describe Krishna in his youth frolicking with adoring girls:

> The cowgirls in pairs joined hands and Krishna was in their midst. Each thought he was at her side and did not recognize them near anyone else. They put their fingers in his fingers and whirled about with rapturous delight.[35]

Although occurring in a group, this experience was essentially dyadic for each of the girls involved.

Krishna is an idealized partner, an incarnation of the god Vishnu. The cowgirls danced with him and loved him as though he were real, but his appearances were surrounded by miraculous events. Time spent with him was not noticed by the rest of the world. Frequently real people are used in similar ways, that is, are perceived for their abstract rather than real qualities. Many a lover idealizes his beloved to the point of worship. This, like involvement with a deity, is not a total dyad. In true dyadic relating, both partners accept the other in his full Personhood.

Dyadic is more complex than solitary ecstasy. Because of the difficulty in developing truly symmetrical relationships—pairs of balanced equals—ecstatic pairing rarely becomes a traditional Way. Instead, asymmetrical pairs of teacher and student are used as vehicles for mystical experience. The Other, the human object, is more fluid and unstable than traditional objects of meditation. Swami Satchidananda thus writes:

> It is very difficult to worship the guru. There is ample opportunity to lose faith in him, while there is nothing to make you lose faith in a picture, a form, a statue of a god. When you adore a living person he is not the same always.[36]

The typical lover is even more unstable than the guru. Lovers choose each other for the sense of excitement or completion they experience together. They do not necessarily see themselves as equals. Their intense union may be based on neurotic needs. Nevertheless, human love has the potential for carrying an individual into an ecstatic state of merger with the Other.

In the dyadic mode, the relationship with the other person is the discipline. People are not dependable in the same way as gods, idols, and ideas. They serve profound interpersonal needs such as dependency and security. They relate in unexpected ways, make threatening demands, have needs of their own. Even in an ecstatic merger through sex, which is biologically geared to pairing, there is still an enormous difficulty in developing a dyadic relationship capable of supporting and maintaining ecstatic experience. Cultures work hard to supply specific roles for people so that their necessary relationships will function smoothly, but in our society these traditional patterns have broken down. Pairs have to work out their own roles and strive to gain an apprehension of the full personhood of the Other. They have to work as hard as any other ecstatic discipline, but without the help of a religious discipline, a dogma, or a formal creed.

The third fundamental ecstatic orientation is that of groups. Like the dyadic orientation, this one also uses the presence of other people to catalyze the dissolution of the "I" and the merger experience. Merger with a single Other in the dyad is frightening for many individuals. It requires trust of oneself and the Other. It frequently takes the partners beyond the clear definition of established roles and into the unpredictable realm of full personhood, which includes infantile dependence as well as mature caring. Groups, on the other hand, provide their members with roles. There is not enough time to explore all the aspects of each member. Certain values are exaggerated, others suppressed. The member gives over his individuality, but he may find it easy to feel safe in the larger organism. He may feel engulfed by a single Other who may threaten to penetrate aspects of his personhood that he wants hidden. The group is more likely to be predictable, to explore only predetermined ritual and ceremonial patterns.

Psychological theorists such as Bion[37] have described a "group-consciousness" phenomenon. They postulate that every group has cognitive and emotional functions that go beyond the contribution of all of its members. In other words, the mere presence of others seems to facilitate sharing thoughts and emotions that are more usually considered an individual possession. The more intense the group, the greater this sense of sharing. Individual identity and social roles are lost and the group mentality becomes the predominant reality. The group mood controls the individual's experience; the group needs dictate his behavior and roles; the group beliefs become his beliefs.

Group-oriented individuals seek out events in which they can experience the sense of union and merger that is the hallmark of ecstasy. All of us participate in such events even if we do not realize that we are seeking an altered subjectivity. Examples in everyday experience are ubiquitous: dance halls, political rallies, fiestas, sports events (for both participants and spectators), communal sings, evangelistic rallies, weekend retreats, student sit-ins, and marathon therapy sessions. All are group events in which the psychology of group merger enables a change in consciousness. Rites of passage such as birth, marriage, and death are often marked by ceremonies in which the group experience calls attention to the moment. Alcohol, drugs, ritual sex, repetitive rhythmic dancing, and pounding music are all technical accessories which facilitate and intensify group merger. Group events unite the members; members who refuse to participate in the larger reality of the community are isolated and treated as scapegoats.

Few groups are truly democratic, that is, rely on the equal participation of the members. Instead they tend to structure the membership into complementary roles. Leaders may need special training, but the mass of followers usually needs remarkably little skill or discipline to reach an ecstatic state in this mode. The energy of a large group is generally so intense that even an uninitiated member can get caught up in the movement and identify with the basic emotions as though they were his own. This is the glory but also the danger of group orientation.

Mass ecstasies are often focussed through a single charismatic individual who has followed rigorous training (generally of an isolated mode) to develop an ability to attain remarkable trance states. The rest of the group moves into an altered state by identifying with the leader either in direct dyadic encounter or mass infection. Shamanism is the name given to religions which use highly trained individuals to communicate with the spirit world for other members of the society. The shaman has often shown an ability to enter trances as a child and has been groomed and tutored in techniques appropriate to the group beliefs. The goal is to enter a state of consciousness in which the shaman is in union with the powers the tribe wants influenced.

Some societies believe in possession by a spirit even if the shaman has no recall of the ecstatic state. Others interpret the trance not as the arrival of an alien spirit, but rather as the departure of the individual's soul (or at least part of the soul) to a spirit world. There are many cases in which the individual experiences and has full recall of conversations or union with spirits or forces.

Mediums at seances are essentially shamans who enter trance states in which they can see or hear spirits from the "other" world, whose messages they "mediate," that is, convey to someone else. Contact with spirits often takes the form of sexual intercourse, a union which may even be formalized with a certificate of marriage. In a society which sanctions shamanistic activity, an official shaman is legitimized and distinguished from the uncontrolled activities of a non-licensed practitioner. The erotic implications of marriage may be acted out through dances in which the mortal partner goes through the motions of love making with his invisible spouse.

From a sociological perspective, the shaman is an eccentric loner whose strange behavior is tolerated in return for his periodic services as ecstatic medium for the larger group. At the beginning of a ritual, the group participates vicariously in the expert performance. Through this leadership and the group experience, they gradually shed their passivity. Group involvement follows the methods of a culture, often including rhythmic music, chanting, swaying, and dancing. Intense ecstatic rituals are particularly effective as initiation rites in which the initiate experiences abreaction and emerges with a new sense of self, a new belief, a feeling of total belonging.

Fernandez has described the state of "one-heartedness"

achieved by members of the tribe he was studying after they had danced all night together and were about to partake of a communal meal.[38] The same phenomenon was observed in a Siberian tribe by Shirokogoroff, writing in 1935:

> The rhythmic music and singing, and later the dancing of the shaman, gradually involve every participant more and more in a collective action. When the audience begins to repeat the refrains together with the assistants, only those who are defective fail to join in the chorus. The tempo of the action increases, the shaman with a spirit is no more an ordinary man or relative, but is a 'placing' (i.e. incarnation) of the spirit; the spirit acts together with the audience and this is felt by everyone. The state of many participants is now near to that of the shaman himself, and only a strong belief that when the shaman is there the spirit may only enter him, restrains the participants from being possessed in mass by the spirit. This is a very important condition of the shamanizing which does not however reduce mass susceptibility to the suggestion, hallucinations and unconscious acts produced in a state of mass ecstasy. When the shaman feels that the audience is with him and follows him he becomes still more active and this effect is transmitted to his audience. After shamanizing, the audience recollects various moments of the performance, their great psychophysiological emotion and the hallucinations of sight and hearing which they have experienced. They then have a deep satisfaction—much greater than that from emotions produced by theatrical and musical performances, literature and general artistic phenomena of the European complex, because in shamanizing the audience at the same time acts and participates.[39]

Group-ecstatic orientation is plagued by charlatanism. The pivotal role of the shaman leader often leads to a demand for performance from an expectant and passive audience. Ecstasy on demand makes a mockery of the entire experience and many practitioners soon become skillful actors in order to maintain their positions. As every thespian knows, the line between simulation and meaningful experience is thin.

For example, a former revivalist preacher in the United States, Marjoe, returned to his "calling" in order to film meetings and make a documentary exposé of the fraud common among circuit preachers. He knew that the film crew was present and that he was preaching as a hypocrite with no conviction in the system of belief that was at the basis of his method; and yet he got caught up and turned on while preaching. He was able to trigger seizures in others, complete with spasms and speaking in tongues, even while he maintained a cynical attitude toward their faith. He did not condemn their behavior, however. He seemed to feel that "getting it on" was a positive goal, but that people should not be exploited. His own conscious intention to expose hypocrisy did not preclude his getting caught up in the rhythms of the preaching and even in the images and beliefs he had been hearing and using since early childhood. It is probable that the old words, old methods, and old environments were heavy cues for him to enter a trance state much as proficient actors use sad memories to induce strong emotional states.

The line between holy man and actor is thin indeed. Although the group aura may superficially facilitate the shaman's ecstasy-producing role, it also robs him of his own experience. Perhaps that is why shamanistic cults and natural botanical hallucinogens have been so closely associated. R. Gordon Wasson suggests that most enduring shamanistic religions relied on hallucinogens either for their one member who occupied the shaman's role or for the entire group.[40] This is not to argue that their ecstasies require the drug experience. There is, for example, a shamanistic ecstasy among the Warac Indians of Venezuela which uses ordinary, non-hallucinogenic tobacco as other cultures use peyote, and with the same psychedelic effect. But group-ecstatic orientation may resort to more direct stimulation of at least some of its members instead of making use of the discipline of solitary mystics.

Group-ecstatic orientation is both complex and controversial. The boundary between the intimacy of the primary family group and the murderous chauvinism of an entire nation is critical to us all. Merger experience requires trust, yet in a group of many people, knowledge of one another can only be superficial. Group trust often becomes an illusion. Leaders are picked for their inspirational or paternal qualities. The same individual who is deified on one occasion may be Satanized on another. Groups may provide a haven for the individual and a relatively easy way to be caught up in a transcendent experience with little effort or specialized skill. However, the danger of the jihad, the holy war, is ever present. Rich, harmonious group ecstasies can too easily become rampant mobs and disciplined armies. The subject is an extremely important one, although it is beyond the scope of this book.

The concept of ecstatic orientation and its classification into solitary, dyadic, and group modes is one of many frames of reference with which to bound a limitless subject. It focusses on the kinds of interactions that stimulate the ecstatic experience. Each of the orientations is a convenient shorthand for those relationships which support or inhibit the development of ecstasy in each of us. The solitary mode eschews relationships entirely. Those who choose this Way begin by detaching themselves from others. The dyadic and group modes use a particular interactional form as a springboard to transcend the ordinary levels of interaction and achieve the merger state.

The cost of throwing off ordinary ways of relating can be very high for the individual. Bonds of one sort or another are absolutely essential for physical and emotional survival. Ecstatic traditions have grown up in almost every culture in order to provide a social framework within which individuals can seek special ways of relating which do not conflict with their ecstatic goals. Monks, for example, belong to orders which subtly support dependency needs until the initiate is able to take up a teaching role in the capacity of master. Rituals may suspend ordinary codes of behavior, even the most basic sexual morality, in the service of a group's ecstatic needs.

It is in dyadic orientation, the most interactive and intimate form, that the tension between ecstasy and relationships is clearest. Love relationships inevitably force real as well as transcendent knowledge of the Other. Most mystical leaders and ecstatic traditions, even those especially directed toward the dyadic orientation, have seen this duality as a threat requiring defenses rather than as a potential to be nourished. In the next chapter we shall examine the traditional pattern of these defenses against human love.

3

The Dyad in Ecstatic Traditions

EACH society legitimizes certain kinds of ecstatic experience and denies others. Ecstasy is seldom allowed to diffuse through members of the society at random. In shamanistic societies, ancient and modern, ecstasy is focussed through certain "holy" members of the society who contain it within restricted ceremonies and specific institutionalized religions. In some cultures, ecstasy becomes an important goal of education, even in earliest childhood; in others, it is censured because it conflicts with "productive" goals. Whatever form the society evolves, the individual subjective experience is so intense that some members choose to make the pursuit of ecstasy their life's work. They may become priests or poets, healers or contemplatives; they may serve or be ostracized. What they have in common is not their role in society so much as their individual quest for frequent and prolonged ecstatic experience.

The permanent decision to center a life style in the pursuit of ecstasy, including the development of modes of relationship conducive to such a pursuit, is a different thing altogether from the brief appreciation of a transient ecstatic experience. All of us know of ecstasy. Even during the first few years of a child's life, when behavior is not accompanied by verbal reports or memories, we can imagine that an ecstatic experience is taking place in the total joyous shiver of the hugging infant or in the profound euphoria of the toddler at play. For many children, these experiences are a cul-de-sac, peripheral to their development. For others, however, they become the goal of life. C. S. Lewis has described these moments as leaving him with "an unsatisfied desire which is itself more desirable than any other satisfaction." In his autobiography *Surprised by Joy*, he points out how his childhood moments of "joy" challenged him at every moment where a lesser emotional experience was more practical or politic. "I doubt," he says, "whether anyone who has tasted it would ever, if both were in his power, exchange it for all the pleasures in the world." [1]

Many people do choose, however, to avoid these surges of "joy." For example, a successful young scientist, married and with children to support, confessed that as an adolescent he would suddenly experience himself as being in a sublime landscape, suffused with joy, which he recognized as the area he had lived in during infancy. He believed that the emotions he felt at these times were the most intense and pleasurable of his life; yet he stopped having these extraordinarily satisfying visions while in his late teens. Rather he decided to follow the demands of a secular life style. He remains afraid of psychedelic drugs, suspecting that they might lead him back to this ecstatic experience and that he might decide never to come back from it. He concerns himself with observable truths about reality, but considers himself vaguely "religious." His is probably the more common history than C. S. Lewis's, but it is less likely to be known. As he admitted, he had never told anyone about these things before. He is only one of an untold number of "closet mystics," simultaneously confused, intrigued, and frightened by their secret knowledge of their "other world."

Those who act on their flashes of extraordinary experience, who seek to develop them rather than to pursue the mundane, are candidates for sainthood. Gautama Buddha's legendary first trance took place under a rose apple tree during a picnic when he was sixteen. He had retreated from the general merriment to dwell on man's pathos and the unity of all life. Gradually, his thoughts moved into the quiet place of peace and ecstasy which is familiar to those who meditate. Legend says that as the hours passed, the shadow of the tree did not move because it did not want to distract the young prince in his quest. The glimpse of ecstasy in his youth stayed with him through the subsequent years of rigid asceticism; it was his assurance that nirvana was ultimately attainable.[2]

For most people, a single, sudden glimpse is not enough to create a devout life style. Timothy Leary and his colleagues had hoped to transform an entire generation to the pursuit of the ecstatic and the mystical and to establish values and an educational system which would further this pursuit. While millions of Americans are "turned on" by psychedelic drugs, only a tiny number permanently change the direction of their lives and devote themselves to a mystic Way. Mystical societies in India have been familiar with intoxicants for inducing trance states for thousands of years, but Eastern culture generally places a disciplined approach to *samadhi* in a quite different category from escapism. Instant ecstasy may provide the door to a new perception of reality or a glance into a new form of consciousness, but nothing more. Developed ecstatic traditions go beyond the mastery of techniques toward the adoption of a suitable way of life to support the quest for ecstasy. In each tradition it is understood that the road is hard, and most fall by the wayside, but that the goal (satori, samadhi, nirvana, cosmic consciousness, omega) is worth the struggle.

What is it in the individual and the group that determines whether the ecstatic path is pursued, whether a childhood "stab of joy" becomes either a landmark on a continuous journey or a forgotten incident? Anecdotal biographies of those who have made the journey provide some superficial answers. They expose a general developmental pattern: a profound childhood experience, forgotten in secular existence until the moment of re-illumination, and the final decision to cast off mundane struggles in pursuit of the transcendent. But behind this scenario is a more meaningful statement about *a decision to embark on a life in a special relationship to other people.* The seeker acknowledges his ability and desire to give up certain kinds of relationships, to live outside the usual kinds of social intercourse. More than any other special trait, *the difference between an ecstatic tradition and instant ecstasy is the presence of special rules about human relationships which define a way of life rather than a single, unintegrated moment.* And on a deeper level still, the decision and ability of an individual to change the usual social pattern of relationships in order to seek the ecstatic way generally reveals a unique experience with relationships, particularly during the formative years of childhood and in the most profound love relationships of adulthood.

In most ecstatic traditions there is a central person who is a Guide for others who seek the ecstatic way. Each tradition has a different name and slightly different function and explanation for these people, but their roles are remarkably constant from culture to culture. Tzaddic, master, shaman, teacher, father, prophet, seeker—all of them are men who have struggled for enlightenment. They have mastered the specific "techniques" of their Way. The techniques (predominantly those of solitary orientation) may be prayer, meditation, fasting, intoxication, paradox, or ritual. Sometimes, as in the case of the shaman, the guides are overtly delegated by their groups to be the medium between the Sacred and the Profane. Not only do they lead the human soul toward perfection, they also mediate between the spirit world and the mortal world in ways appropriate to the belief system of the culture. Even without a formal shamanistic mission, they have license to speak and act in extraordinary poetic or symbolic ways and thus express the spiritual and mystical needs of other members of their group.

Many cultures explicitly use a journey through spirit regions as the central spiritual event to test the initiate. Usually under the influence of drugs, the would-be shaman experiences a long and arduous trip during which he overcomes monstrous spirits and ultimately reaches a region in which some special knowledge or meaning is waiting. Societies with an elaborate ecstatic tradition or a carefully structured apprenticeship system provide an expectation for the initiate. Don Juan, the teacher to whom Carlos Castaneda went for instruction, identified the ominous figures seen by his student as "aliens."[3] In other cultures, the expectation is that the traveller will meet the spirits of his ancestors:

When I ate *eboka,* I found myself taken by it up a long road in a deep forest until I came to a barrier of black iron. At that barrier, unable to pass, I saw a crowd of black persons also unable to pass. In the distance beyond the barrier it was very bright. I could see many colors in the air but the crowd of black people could not pass. Suddenly my father descended from above in the form of a bird. He gave to me then my *eboka* name, Onwan Misengue, and enabled me to fly up after him over the barrier of iron. As we proceeded, the bird who was my father changed from black to white—first his tail feathers, then all his plumage. We came then to a river the color of blood in the midst of which was a great snake of three colors . . . I looked up and saw a woman in the moon—a bayonet was piercing her heart from which a bright white fire was pouring forth. Then I felt a pain on my shoulder. My father told me to return to earth. I had gone far enough. If I went further, I would not return.[4]

The relationship of the guide to the seeker is not generally taken to be part of the ecstatic path; it is not thought of as a dyadic merger. The teacher must lead the student to his own encounter, to his own conquest of fear or attainment of wisdom—or failure. Some psychotherapists see themselves in this role, leading their patients through the nightmare landscape of their souls, confronting the monsters of their anxiety and hatred, and finally reaching the wisdom of insight.

The men who devote their lives to an ecstatic path rarely do so in order to find a special role in society. They see their world as different from others, and their journeys take them far afield from the life styles common to the culture. Nevertheless, particularly in societies which institutionalize spiritual paths, special knowledge of the spirit world (or of the unconscious, archetypes, or other modern terminology) gives the guides, gurus, teachers, or therapists special roles. Often they are not allowed to mingle with other people in everyday activities. They are placed in some special relationship to an ideal order.

A very few of these individuals become great spiritual leaders, individuals whose wisdom profoundly touches not only the souls of their contemporaries, but also influences the thinking of subsequent generations. Such leaders, the innovative mystics, often share a life style that transcends the habits of the country of their origin. They tend toward a similar pattern of human relating. The Hasidic master Bal Shem Tov is a typical example. He was capable of rapt meditation, mystical incantation, endless feats of prayer, fantastic exercises in silent concentration, soaring flights of mystical ecstasy while communing with God. He was a great teacher, but also, and as profoundly, he was a wanderer and a solitary. He gathered followers around him, but he was not attached to any of them. His was the solitary mode par excellence. He related to the sacred in the universe rather than to the mundane in man. He was more comfortable with children than with adults, but he preferred to be alone. It took an effort to relate to people, but that was the price he had to pay to plant his ideas, his truths, in others. He was worshipped and loved by his disciples, but he held himself aloof.

Many of the other prophets—Jesus, Gautama, Ramakrishna, Gurdjieff—reveal the same pattern. They were masters of their techniques and their messages. They collected and taught disciples. But they remained alone and aloof from human relationships. And when they were not burdened with leadership, they went off alone to commune with silence and the Other Reality. They acted as if people held them back from their personal search for the ecstatic infinite.

Sometimes this other-worldly quality in their relating patterns created human suffering in the name of the sacred mission. The Hasidic masters almost to a man abandoned their wives (whom they married through arrangement in their early teens) and thereafter remained free of close ties. Gandhi did the same. Christian and Buddhist monasteries and nunneries institutionalize a disassociation from family or other intimate bonds for those who really desire to search for Christ or nirvana. Leaders in recent humanistic-ecstatic traditions in the United States are also showing a trend toward divorce, as if marriage and long-term intimate relationships are impediments to personal spiritual growth.

The biography of Gautama Buddha, the revered teacher and God of the Buddhist faith, illustrates this attitude. As a youth Gautama was surrounded by beauty and luxury. His family hoped to bring him out of his contemplative withdrawal and involve him in the working of the world by having him marry young. The marriage was a good one for ten years; his wife Yasodhara has even been characterized as a companion from earlier incarnations. But Gautama was disturbed by the luxurious qualities of his life. When he was told that he was the father of a son, he knew he had to leave. He had a sudden realization of how engrossing it would be to care for a family. He named his son Rahula, fetter, for he saw him as yet another relationship, another bond which he must cut. He looked in briefly on his sleeping wife and baby, then left the palace on his quest.

Gautama drew other young men from their marital security. When he was established as a famous monk, he attended the wedding of his step-brother Nanda. When the groom came out into a grove to meet Gautama and return a begging bowl which the monk had left with him, Gautama interpreted the gesture as a desire to enter the religious order and ordained him on the spot. Much later, when Rahula too had become a monk, Gautama's father came to rebuke him for taking young men from their families. Gautama was apparently moved by the truth of this fact, for he formulated a rule that a son may not join the order without the express permission of his mother and father.

It is not unusual for an individual to suffer great personal loss immediately before embarking on a mission to sainthood. A new way of life often appears to substitute the general love of man, God, or the universe for the more specific love of a spouse or other loved one who has caused some pain. The life of Swami Satchidananda is prototypical. The son of a wealthy landowner, he lived his younger years as a successful business innovator with a deep but contained spiritual inclination. He knew that marriage was an act of worldly involvement: "I loved my wife, but at the same time I wasn't attached to her." [5] The couple had two sons, but the husband was continually haunted by premonitions that his wife would die. After five years, she did die. His thoughts turned increasingly to other-worldly matters. He lost interest in business and finally left his children with his mother and became a monk.

The move toward the ecstatic seems to correspond with a need to retreat from intense, long-term relationships with others and with a devotion to freedom from possessing or being possessed. No matter what route toward the loss of the "I" is taken, long-term relationships seem to act as constraints on the soul's flight into the infinite. They are discouraged or forbidden to most who become masters.

Yoga is typical of ecstatic traditions that institutionalize taboos on relationships. Disciples of this Way reject the profane aspects of existence and embrace the sacred. They seek an ultimate reality in which "object" identifies itself completely with "subject." In yoga's highest form, there is no compromise; it insists on a total abnegation of worldly aspects of bodily relationships, and even of existence. The cosmic illusions of personality and personal experience are endured along the way only because they are vehicles of an appreciation of man's true state. Once man realizes his true condition, he is reborn into a new state of freedom. When he has reached this enlightenment, he finds a sacred world, a new mode of being that is inaccessible to the profane level of existence. The route to enlightenment is a long series of refusals. All aspects of normal existence are stripped away. The most threatening and difficult obstacle for the yogi to overcome is the unconscious dynamism, the psychological potential toward love and life which is activated by "profane" contacts with people who assert personality and value mortal interactions.

In yoga, relationships are said to feed the cosmic illusion. They reinforce the notion of individual specialness and the false continuity of an individual identity. Relationships are denigrated as part of the Maya, the false matrices of man that must be rejected. As Gurdjieff points out in his own system:

> One of man's important mistakes is his illusion in regard to his "I." His "I" changes as quickly as his thoughts, feelings, and moods, and he makes a profound mistake in considering himself always one and the same person; in reality he is always a different persona, not the one he was a moment ago. Man has no permanent and unchangeable "I." [6]

If the loss of the "I" is a requirement of achieving the final goal of freedom, then personal relationships are inhibiting, for it is the Other that helps one to recognize the "I." Separated from meaningful others, the "I" loses importance and eventually disappears. The focus shifts from the specialness of a person in individual or group relationships to the universality of self in harmony with the cosmos.

Psychological needs for intimacy and closeness are perhaps the hardest aspects of profane involvement to give up. To counter-act the continual threat of love and relationship, yoga (like other ecstatic traditions) provides ways for such secular relationships as family bonds to be gradually replaced by a more diffuse group communality. Participation consists in commitment to a movement and its ethos and participating with others who agree on the same point of view. The community shares a variety of good works emphasizing selflessness and asceticism in combination with what Eliade calls "techniques for autonomy"—prayer, physical exercise, fasting, meditation, and solitude. And yet, despite an increasing psychic isolation from others, there is one profound dyadic relationship that supports and motivates the entire process. One human relationship stays central, the tie between the initiate and his guru—and yet this relationship is part of a paradox.

In the yoga tradition, the guru is the wise man, the guide, the holy one. His every act is geared toward remaining free from attachment. His way of relating provides a model for this freedom. He teaches by example how to circumvent and negate such temptations of human contact as dependency, dominance, and sexuality. The student must concentrate on the guru's image, not on his personhood, during the stripping-away process that leads toward enlightenment. Ultimately, the teacher must shatter the "illusion" of their special bond. The relationship can stand only as long as the loss of the "I" is furthered. As long as it is based on the illusion of the uniqueness of the teacher and his relationship with the student, it is an impediment which must be transcended if samadhi is to be reached.

> The teaching mission of the guru is an attempt to *free his followers from him.* His metaphors and parables make it necessary for the pilgrims who would be disciples to turn to their own imaginations in the search for meaning in their lives. The guru instructs the pilgrims in the tradition of breaking with tradition, in losing themselves so that they may find themselves.[7]

The koan, the traditional parable of Zen, is symbolic of the relationship between the Zen master and his pupils. It forces the student to give up searching for understanding by seeing that there is nothing to be understood, and it also teaches him to stop searching for someone to assist him in finding fulfillment. The tales of the Hasidim fulfill the same double function. They provide wisdom by turning the questioner back on himself and deny him the convenience of a wise man who knows all the answers.

The more the guru negates his own person and his own capacity to provide answers, the more the student is forced to give up *his* search for personal power. It is particularly difficult for the student to accept the fact that the guru himself is involved in the struggle for an ego-less state. He may conceptualize the guru as a perfect embodiment of the sacred and try to gain samadhi by identifying with him. But in so doing he remains dependent on another mortal instead of shaking free of all ties. Many disciples thus fail to go beyond the illusion of individual specialness. They transform their relationships with the guru into religious worship. Their feelings of awe and reverence and ecstatic intimacy are ascribed not to a person, but to his immortal role. The teacher becomes a manifestation of the fixed and immutable Godhead.

When the essential principle behind the techniques of ecstatic traditions is analyzed, it becomes clear why disciples must be removed from close personal contacts except for carefully regulated encounters with the guru. The goal is to break free from reality-bound "illusions" and egocentric consciousness toward a higher state in which only universal and timeless truths are of importance. At the heart of all techniques, exercises, prayers, frenzy, or meditation is the same attempt to reach a state of consciousness in which the all and the nothing are one, in which unity, totality, and absence of "I" completely consume one's being. Techniques of concentration, objects of worship, and rituals all act to direct the energy of the ego outside of its usual sphere. The individual strives to become absolutely absorbed in the single object or action chosen as a vehicle. To reach the end state he must achieve absolute absorption in his technique. The discipline of ecstatic traditions consists in learning to focus upon the ecstasy-inducing technique, to break down the personal boundary which ordinarily encloses differences between self and world and participate in a merger or union with the object of concentration or with the people who constitute the ritual group. This union leads to the experience of total merger with the universe. If I am the blue vase, or if I am my breathing, or if I am the group, then I am also the mountain, an atom, or the universe itself.

"I am the Other" is the way of the ecstatic dyad. But the real relationship must be put aside, too, or it will intrude upon the progression of consciousness toward selflessness and merger with the universe. For example, what happens if, deep in meditation and on the threshold of a freer state, the devout is called by name? Naming is the very essence of individuality and uniqueness. A name generally relates to a person's alert, interactive level of consciousness. It makes one distinct in the universe. It can be used to call one back from solitary ecstasy.

What the ecstatic traditions have institutionalized is a way to prevent ordinary teaching, even loving, relationships from intruding upon the individual in search of a life filled with ecstasy. That is not to say that such a life is possible only within the confines of a cult. There are many whose ecstatic orientation and skills require other kinds of interactions than those which are fulfilled by the monastery or ashram or periodic group orgy. As Shakespeare observed, "The poet, the madman, and the lover are of imagination all compact." [8] These three kinds of men are labelled by society as "other" and yet they do not follow the disciplines of a special order. They are in a sense secular mystics who attempt to live out their lives as normal men. Shakespeare had in mind people who seem so intensely absorbed in their own inner world that they had neither time nor interest in external events—men like Hamlet or Macbeth, wrapped up in an internal experience over which they seemed to have little control. Creative artists must interact in the real world intensely enough to be capable of transforming everyday occurrences into transcendent images. They cannot easily retreat from the profane world without losing the raw material of their creations. Shakespeare wrote his greatest plays while serving as an actor/owner of a theater company. Similarly, many artists have been involved in the political life of their country—Plato, Milton, Solzhenitsyn, to name just a few. And yet an artist's real interactions must also be limited or else his other reality may be obscured. Societies learn to make certain allowances for artists (as they do for the madman and the shaman) in return for the vicarious experience produced by the art.

Artists are allowed privileges of behavior; they are even

expected to have eccentricities of dress and manner. But the artist can seldom find for himself a world as protected and as ideally constructed for the induction of his ecstatic states as the monk's. Each artist must struggle for his own style and must operate in connection with the world for his material. He may have a tradition and he may find a great teacher, but he must learn to focus on a product even while he is working on an ecstatic state. He must learn simultaneously to transcend the self-conscious "I" and express his most honest awareness of reality in a style true to his "self." Similarly, the lover cannot experience ecstasy in isolation. His dyadic orientation requires another person and real communication within a viable relationship if the ecstasy is to be more than a momentary flash. He has no product, but he has an object with which he must interact. He does not withdraw from the world, but he tries to continue to live his life from day to day, almost as usual. As Buber remarks:

> The I is indispensable for any relationship, including the highest, which always presupposes an I and You. What has to be given up is not the I but that false drive for self-affirmation which impels man to flee from the unreliable, unsolid, unlasting, dangerous world of relation into the having of things.[9]

The trick is to give up "that false drive for self-affirmation" without giving up all sense of that "self" which transcends the "I," a situation which is essentially paradoxical and inexplicable, but real nevertheless.

While the experience of love is often considered ecstatic, it is rarely thought to be an ecstatic tradition. "Falling in love" is perceived to be an instant ecstasy similar to the ten hours of mystic visions that may follow the intake of LSD. The ecstasy of sex may take place within a relationship; intimacy with another may provide the opportunity for a variety of ecstatic experiences. But relationships themselves are rarely viewed as the core of an ecstatic experience. We seem concerned only with the question of how to design a relationship which does *not prevent* the individual's solitary quest for his own way. It rarely occurs to us to make the relationship itself the disciplined route to ecstatic experience.

Despite the current ambivalence about love as a route to ecstasy, our culture does have some traditional ecstatic love relationships in which special sectors of life-cycle relationships are isolated from ordinary intercourse and made sacred. For example, we have idealized the mother/infant bond as the subject of both art and religion. The beatific Madonna and Child are in sharp contrast with the infant "mewling and puking" in its mother's arms. An idealized projection sublimates (that is, makes sublime) real events. It is a distortion, but it also reflects the truth of the profound ecstatic emotions originating within the mother/infant relationship. Similarly, the sexual relationships of adolescent lovers have been sublimated into a tradition of romantic love which is manifested in our extraordinary worship of the young and the beautiful. This idealization projects the beauty of the experience but conceals the imperfections of most lovers' bodies and the imperfect fusion of their souls.

In fact, most "love traditions" (including our own romantic tradition) tend to exclude a consideration of the total spectrum of the relationship—sexual, spiritual, and interpersonal—in favor of a narrower and less fettered point of view. In some traditions, sex is made cosmic rather than personal, spiritual rather than organic, even though the physical body and the sexual organs are part of the Way to transcendent experience. In an introduction to the Kama Sutra, John Spellman writes:

> Mankind is endlessly involved in the complexities of life. These are annoying, puzzling, and frustrating. He therefore seeks some common element which he is certain must connect all things and thus produce that security of unity for which he longs. . . . Love then becomes a yearning for union with the divinity. From this, it is but a step to have the sex act itself considered as a symbolic union in which the participants represent certain cosmic principles. The power and mystery of creation is worshipped using the sexual organs as symbols.[10]

Sex is thus made into a cosmic force and myth which may or may not be related to sexual intercourse with another human. In practice this leads to the remarkable series of sexual encounters in the tradition of Tantra Yoga in which sexual activity is stereotyped to conform to a sacramental union. Tantra Yoga has certain parallels to romantic love, for in its system man and woman achieve ecstatic bliss through contact with each other. The training, however, is geared to reduce the individuality of both participants, particularly of the woman. She is taught to appear to the male celebrant as the incarnation of the female principle, Shakti; he becomes the male god, Shiva.

Tantra is closer to the solitary orientation than a true dyadic tradition. It is basically a meditative technique which requires months of preparation on the part of the practitioners. Before culminating in *maithuna*, a ritual sexual union, the couple must independently practice subtle yoga exercises which include breathing, prayer, and the gradual intensification of sensory perception. They must purify the psyche and develop a flow of energy from higher planes. *Maithuna* itself takes place under carefully controlled circumstances and according to carefully established rules which include a ritual bath and a ritual meal as well as ritual sexual union. Penetration is not allowed until both partners lose their real image and take the form of a god or goddess. The entire ceremony of *maithuna* is designed to obliterate the carnal and secular relationship. "The sadhaka gazes upon her with admiration and awe, as one pondering the mystery of creation and the unfathomable secret of being." [11] If the *sadhaka* (male) cannot accomplish this vision and identify himself with the cosmic union of Shiva-Shakti, he must not proceed, for he would merely be indulging in a carnal act of sexual intercourse. If he goes on, every movement is codified:

> Deep penetration of the vagina at this point is neither necessary nor desirable. But close contact between the lingam (penis) and the moist membrane of the inner yoni (vagina) is important. The sadhaka (male) and his consort now lie completely motionless and relaxed for a period

of 32 minutes. During this interval, the co-partners visualize the flow of pranic currents between them, the strongest being at the point of contact between the sexual organs. A sudden acme of sensations occurs at some point between the 28th and 32nd minute of practice. This abrupt excitation, unlike anything ever experienced before, results in orgiastic and involuntary contraction of the body's total musculature . . .

A clearly perceived decrease of tension follows, as the direction of the pranic currents is reversed, now flowing inward rather than outward, entering the nadis of the subtle body and energizing the entire organism.[12]

When conducted successfully, *maithuna* brings union:

The maithuna couple become as a single principle of being. They return to the latent condition of Brahman, wherein there is Atmarama or play of the self with the self.[13]

In Platonic thought, the beloved inspires the lover to a fresh vision of the Reality that lies beyond our mortal vision. Socrates suggests that each man chooses his beloved according to his ability to evoke a sense of that Reality in the lover. As in Tantra Yoga, the beloved is taken primarily as a symbol of another world. He is loved for those qualities that are most abstract and least personal.[14]

According to the Greek ideal of beauty, the beloved was a young man, not a woman. The term "Greek love" is sometimes used to mean male homosexuality. The ideal that inspired Socrates to a sense of union with the sublime led other Greeks to court young men in the gymnasium. Upper-class Greek society made a sharp distinction between the rearing of boys and of girls. They were trained for different interests and different life styles. When they married, their relationship was directed toward procreation and household management. The marital relationship—or indeed any man-woman relationship—was not regarded as a means for attaining bliss.

When women have an idealized place in society, they may become the object of ecstatic love. Europe in the late Middle Ages provides an extreme example. Noble women were often left in charge of large castles while their husbands were away on crusades or on some other dangerous and prolonged mission. These women were obliged to provide accommodations for travelers in need of shelter. They were well educated and, in addition to their administrative responsibilities, frequently had time to develop an interest in the arts. A class of entertainers grew up who devoted themselves to the patronage of these women. Not surprisingly, the troubadours spoke of the beauty and charm of those who supported their work. Increasingly, the woman was described as an inspiring, desirable, ideal object, capable of transforming the heart and soul of the devoted lover, her servant. Although the troubadours occasionally had sexual relationships with the women of whom they sang with such adoration, the general rule was that the pain and suffering of unrequited love was more sublime than the physical pleasures and harmony of love fulfilled. There was no ideal centered upon any kind of relationship; rather, the ideal was a continual yearning, a continual quest for satisfaction that would never come.

In *Love in the Western World,* Denis de Rougemont points out that the roots of the tradition of courtly love (as propagated by the troubadours) can be traced to Christian heresies inspired by Eastern mystical traditions. De Rougemont further suggests that twelfth-century European knights and troubadours may have been using love as a metaphor for another kind of ecstatic journey. Although the language was that of love, its object was not a real woman, for the lover was not involved with her in any day-to-day relationship. Thus in the stories of Tristan, Lancelot, and the other legendary lovers popular in those times, tragedy results when the hero actually obtains his beloved, when he tastes the favors of the flesh that previously had excited his mystical passion. If his love had remained a metaphor for the path to the divine, his life might have stayed sublime. De Rougemont sees the myth of Tristan and Isolde as the archetype of courtly love, a tradition in which the division between romantic bliss and a practical relationship is particularly sharp.[15]

Throughout the late medieval and Renaissance periods in Europe, romantic love held an ambiguous relationship to marriage. On the one hand, married Christian love was seen as a central force in a balanced view of the universe. Shakespeare's romantic comedies gain their sense of joyous vitality and propriety from happy, almost fairy-tale endings in which all obstacles are overcome and the lovers united. For all their emphasis on propriety and universal order, however, Shakespeare's plays also abound with allusions to extramarital affairs. For every successful, legitimate pairing there is an allusion to cuckolding. After 1660 English drama frequently portrayed the comic involvement of married women with other men. Cuckolding became not just allusive material but a dominant theme. In a typical (if superior) play, *The Country Wife,* the intrigues of a married woman with her lover take on far more interest than the conventional problems of a pair of honest lovers who marry at the end.

Despite our contemporary ethic and economy in which men and women can marry for love, we still tend to believe in the separation of love (as passion) and an enduring relationship. Much of the excitement of love still seems to come from obstacles and illicit intrigues. We are hypocrites in this matter, for we continue to marry romantically even though we do not believe that romantic love can endure in a day-to-day marriage. The courts of twelfth-century France were more honest in this regard, particularly that which issued the following proclamation in 1174:

> We declare and affirm, by the tenor of those present, that love cannot extend its rights over two married persons. For indeed lovers grant one another all things mutually and freely, without being impelled by a motive of necessity whereas husband and wife are held by their duty to submit their wills to each other and to refuse each other nothing. May this judgment, which we have delivered with extreme caution, and after consulting with a great number of other ladies, be for you a constant and unassailable truth, delivered in this year 1174 on the third day before the Kalends of May, proclamation VII.[16]

We continue to believe in the separation of ecstatic relationships from human affairs. That does not mean that we do not value relationships. Quite the contrary, we now have a vast therapeutic apparatus for improving them. Marriage, couple, and family therapy all attempt to analyze and improve the intricacies of communication in relationships. Simultaneously, members of our society are searching for new ways to achieve ecstatic moments in relationships, particularly through sex. We have frank, descriptive books, sex education in the schools, and practical Masters and Johnson sexual therapy. These techniques may be valuable, but they remain a defense against our deep-seated disbelief that two people can really combine communication and sexuality in one long-term ecstatic encounter.

Consider the experience of falling in love. In almost all descriptions of it, a variety of exquisite transcendent feelings are totally separated from the relationship itself. It is probably true that an essential factor in a new love relationship is that there is no true knowledge of the Other. Lovers commune with each other's souls but not with each other's whims, emotions, anxieties, and peculiarities. They incredibly overvalue each other. Beatrice and Juliet do not exist as flesh and blood, but only in a lover's imagination. Ecstatic moments contained in the experience of falling in love fade rapidly when the love object emerges from behind his projected mask. The moment that person becomes real, that stereotyped, flawless perfection is challenged by a whining request, a burp, or an awkward gesture; the moment the real relationship intrudes, the lovers enter a new state which is rarely described as ecstatic. Love is called blind because the lover can refuse to see the unlovely aspects of his beloved. The beloved is like a deity, fixed and immutable. The heights of most love ecstasies occur when contact is still on a fantasy level. Once a relationship develops, the love object no longer remains an idol and ecstatic moments are more difficult to achieve.

Continuing ecstasy in the context of a real relationship (in which each of us has our own history, consciousness, expectations) is an entirely different process from the euphoric creation of an immutable illusion, an idealized beloved. The direction and needs of that process are not spelled out. There is no Way of Love as there is a Way of Buddhism, Zen, Yoga, Hasidism, or mystical Christianity. There are no rules for using a personal relationship as a route to ecstatic bliss or personal wholeness. Most of us are frightened rather than intrigued by the idea of losing our sense of "I" in a dyad with an Other, for that Other may betray our trust.

The paradox of love and ecstasy is the social context. *Other forms of ecstasy move away from the profane day-to-day dynamics of human relationships, but love between two people must take place within a relationship.* Its renewal depends on the continuance of the relationship in a form which supports further ecstatic union or in multiple new relationships with the germ of ecstasy reborn again and again. Mystics shy away from close relationships. Love is an ecstatic route that relies on relationships. Love ecstasy requires the interpersonal form which other ecstatic traditions work so hard to strip away or transmute beyond the human into love of God, nature, the universe, or cosmos.

Why do relationships impinge so strongly on human ecstasy as a way of life and at the same time exist as the repository of the most universal of ecstasies? To be in a relationship with another is to be joined with him, to be connected with him in meaningful ways. It means that, in regard to the relationship, the two are as one. There is no magic in the word "relationship" or in the kinds of human contact that it defines, but there is a statement of a kind of bond which goes beyond a brief liaison or chance encounter. "Relationship" implies mutual obligation, interlocking roles, commitment. It implies that the two function as a unit in certain activities. It is a sociological word which indicates the ways in which one person interacts, communicates, and performs with another.

Relationships can be Platonic, sexual, maternal, loving, holy, sacred, profane, biological, unnatural—they have been given many names which reflect the ideal a culture has for such roles. The reality is generally much more difficult to define. Relationships shift as deeper levels of the individuals come into contact with each other. Relationships are the continued interplay of intangible forces. Society places limits, and establishes ideals, but there can be no real limits upon human contact. There is no constancy or certainty; and there is the continual temptation, offset by occasional anxiety or fear, to go further, to enter hidden wells of the Other and the self, to break through the arbitrary boundaries of what the roles "should" be between the two. It is hard enough to understand ourselves and to control our own behavior; the Other is even more unknowable and even freer from the possibility of control. That is the threat and joy of relating.

When we feel ecstasy in a human relationship we call it love. The experience becomes a personal truth in the same way that the ecstatic bliss of St. Teresa when she was in communion with Christ (which she also called love) was a personal truth. However, the vehicle of St. Teresa's ecstasy rested upon a foundation of immutable doctrine and knowledge of an everlasting God. Her "spiritual betrothal" and all other "holy" relationships were the final fantasy of a constant, enduring relationship. Lovers of mere mortals experience similar emotions, but have a range of problems which the mystic does not have to face. No matter how sure we, as lovers, may be of our own feelings, we can never fully trust the relationship. The relationship we experience may be a transient phenomenon based on passing needs, on roles that will be outgrown, on contact that will soon become impossible. Lovers risk loss in a way that mystics do not.

If the "I" is to be lost, it can be done more safely with an absolute; to merge the "I" with another mortal is dangerous and distracting. When lovers choose to know each other as a complex, fluid, changing essence, as interacting humans, they are rejecting the sure paths that the religions of man have mapped out. They are choosing to risk loss, to risk getting lost in something that is as unsteady as a house of cards, as illusive as a will-o'-the-wisp. They are moving beyond symbol while trying to find ecstasy in reality, meaning in the concrete rather than the abstract. Traditional ecstatic dyads do not deal with whole relationships. They are much closer to the ecstasy of the solitary orientation; the more the ecstatic is pursued, the more the seeker must be purified of social contact. The Other is confronted as a sex object, a symbol, as an unattainable object, as an unsatisfied desire.

Our society is searching for ecstasy in a variety of ways, almost all of them outside of major relationships, particularly those that provide security and comfort. Most of the time, relationships are used to satiate our dependency needs while we search for ecstasy elsewhere (alone or in groups). If we have an ideal of dyadic love, an ideal of marriage, it is one in which both partners try to actuate themselves individually while remaining together as trusting friends, supportive and understanding of what is "right" for the other. Gibran's poem "On Marriage," which has often been used as a text at marriage ceremonies, conveys the spirit of this understanding:

Then Almitra spoke again and said, And what of Marriage,
Master?
And he answered saying:
You were born together, and together you shall be
forevermore!
You shall be together when the white wings of death
scatter your days.
Ay, you shall be together even in the silent memory
of God.
But let there be spaces in your togetherness,
And let the winds of the heavens dance between you.
Love one another, but make not a bond of love:
Let it rather be a moving sea between the shores
of your souls.
Fill each other's cup but drink not from one cup.
Give one another of your bread but eat not from
the same loaf.

Sing and dance together and be joyous, but let each
one of you be alone,
Even as the strings of a lute are alone though they
quiver with the same music.
Give your hearts, but not into each other's keeping.
For only the hand of Life can contain your hearts.
And stand together yet not too near together.
For the pillars of the temple stand apart,
And the oak tree and the cypress grow not in
*each other's shadow.**

Our culture is afraid and distrustful of relationships that focus inwardly, in which two persons become inextricably involved, lost in each other. It expects the partners to seek their own ways, to explore instant ecstasies, other ways to self-fulfillment—to let each other "do their own thing." If one partner will not let the other experiment with extramarital sex, with drugs, with group cults, or with a new job, society tends to support the partner who chooses to dissolve the marriage, who says he has "outgrown" the other. The assumption is that individuals should search in their own ways, then come back with what they have learned and enrich the relationship. Marriage, then, is a secure bond which allows the individual the psychological and emotional freedom to experiment. When it stops functioning that way, it is dissolved.

In this ideal of marriage, once the early love of boy/girl romance fades away, dependency replaces ecstasy as the dominant feeling. When the relationship needs renewal, it tends to come from outside rather than from within. To expect more is to run the risk of being out of date with a changing world in which procreating can be scientific and long-term relationships are designed for security, not ecstasy.

If there is an alternative to the new romantic tradition of Gibran and those who think like him, it is best expressed by

* Reprinted from *The Prophet*, by Kahlil Gibran, with permission of the publisher, Alfred A. Knopf, Inc. Copyright 1923 by Kahlil Gibran; renewal copyright 1951 by administrators C.T.A. of Kahlil Gibran estate and Mary G. Gibran. (Our emphasis—L.C.)

Martin Buber. His belief comes closest to an expression of the sacred potential of the human dyad. He believes that the "I" exists only as "I" experiencing "It" or as "I" relating to an Other, referred to by Buber as *"Du,"* translated as "Thou" or "You." "There is no I as such but only the I of the basic word I-You and the I of the basic word I-It." [17] For Buber, the act of relation is totally reciprocal; love is a feeling between I and Thou which is more than something simply within each; it is a cosmic force. Relationship and love are more than feelings and actions of I and Thou. In a relationship, the I and Thou simultaneously are dependent and free, created and creative. Marriage, then, must go beyond freedom, companionship, and parallel experience:

> Marriage can never be renewed except by that which is always the source of all true marriage: that two human beings reveal the You to one another. It is of this that the You that is I for neither of them builds a marriage. This is the metaphysical and metapsychical fact of love which is merely accompanied by feelings of love.[18]

In other words, Buber believes in a quality of relating that goes beyond standing together; it is a quality in which the two partners lose track of the distinctions between them, in which the I-Thou unit takes the place of the two I's or the two Thou's. It is a true dyad, a group of two which takes its meaning and gets its essence from its existence as a single phenomenon whose two components operate individually only for peripheral events.

It is easy to understand the popularity of Gibran's ethic compared to the abstract ideal of Buber's encounter. There is no ecstasy in Gibran's method, for there is no merger experience. And yet it provides a code of living which fits with our norm of serial polygamy. Today the partners of a marriage do not necessarily stay together. Because of the pain of separation, "wiser" individuals try to establish non-possessive relationships with their new partners. They try to establish a relationship in which freedom rather than fusion is the keystone. They operate openly in separate realms with the understanding that if one or the other needs a friend, becomes a casualty, or needs special caring, the spouse will be there to help.

This vision can well extend to the most stable marriages, which have always required security and friendship more than ecstasy. In the past, marriage was a relatively effective setting in which to raise children. Husband, wife, father, and mother were socially defined roles supported by the extended family and community. In our own day, two people who barely know each other stand alone trying to create all roles for each other. They move every five years, breaking contact with family and friends. They are forced to be friends, work partners, and therapists as well as lovers, and yet they may have few mutual friends and few times to experience themselves as a unit in the eyes of the strangers who live around them or who work with them. External excitement replaces internal discovery. Marriage cannot be a lifelong and effortless love affair when such enormous mutual demands are placed on the partners. When they experience the inevitable diminution of romantic bliss, they either agree to stay together as two strings on a single instrument or they separate. In some communities of California (where the trend toward accelerated marital dissolution appeared earlier than in the rest of the country), it is *unusual* for a school child to have his original set of parents intact. Complicated interlocking visiting privileges become the social environment for childhood development. If the institution of marriage has lost its capacity to provide a secure child-rearing environment, then it has lost much of its cultural sanction. We are realistic when we search for alternate social relationships.

Perhaps Tantra and the tradition of courtly love are wise to divide human interactions into reality-comfort-dependence versus fantasy-ecstasy-romance. For why must everything be put into one context? Long-term relationships are well suited to provide dependency-security needs. Perhaps our search for the ecstatic and transcendent can and should occur elsewhere.

Then what of love and ecstasy? Is ecstasy within the context of a relationship reserved only for the mother-infant pairing, an adolescent crush, a brief affair, or a sexual encounter? Perhaps not. Beyond these brief experiences, these instant ecstasies, there lies an ecstatic potential which need not be merely a metaphor for occult or religious mysteries but is viable in its own right. It is not an easy Way. It does not guarantee results. A joint quest for transcendence is not the same as our human need for closeness or the flash of ecstasy that is a potential part of all intimate encounters; and in the same way transcendental meditation twice a day for fifteen minutes is not the same as meditating sixteen hours a day for fifteen years.

The dyadic orientation, the path of dyadic love, is less precise and less specific than other Ways. Relationships encompass both the day-to-day world of practical interactions and the extraordinary universe of transcendent union. The complexity of social demands often makes the ecstatic aspects of a relationship the byproduct rather than its essence. It is exceedingly difficult to fuse the two worlds of the mundane and the ecstatic, but it is even more difficult to find another real person with whom one can exist both in transcendent experience and in everyday reality. *To attempt to share both levels with another person is to join the quest for an ecstatic mutual way of life.*

Many of us make that quest, but it is not a Way that recommends itself. It has no prophet and no roles, no Buddha, no shaman, and no book. It makes no clear distinction between the sacred and the profane. Yet it is the oldest ecstatic tradition from both a historical and a personal point of view. In the next chapter we will show how love ecstasy shared by two people is the substance from which all other Ways proceed.

4

The Origin of Ecstatic Consciousness

(PRE-RELATIONAL STAGES OF DEVELOPMENT)

THE unfolding of infant consciousness from conception until the age of three can be viewed as the pre-history of the merger experience in man. Infants emerge from the fetal state of physical relationship to a barely more separated condition in which their physical and psychological survival depends completely on others. At first they are at one with the world, enveloped in a universe in which the mother is herself indistinguishable from the rest of existence. Later, within the two-person universe of mother and child, and eventually in the family group, children participate in those successive "pre-relational" merger experiences which lay the psychological foundations for their approaching individuality and sense of "I-ness." It is not until age three that they can begin to live in their families as assertive individuals capable of interacting as separate parts in relationships.

Ecstasy, like the consciousness of an infant, is a merger experience in which the "I" does not exist. In many ways the dynamics of ecstasy reflect and invert the dynamics of infant consciousness. Children struggle to find individuality while mystics seek to lose it. Children search for an identity separate and apart from the world, the dyad, or the group while mystics escape identity in merger through one of these forms.

The concept of merger is a profound metaphor for our origins; it is simultaneously the fact of our origins. We start life as dependent beings fused with the physiology of another person. There is no "I" at the beginning. We do not answer to our own name, the symbol of our separateness, until much later. As adults, we seem committed to a struggle to maintain the illusion of separateness. We compulsively assert that each of us is a unique individual. It can be threatening to our tenuously maintained "I" to admit how much of "I" remains "we." Our language reflects this attitude. Being "grown up" is synonymous with "being on our own." Being mature means to "know who you are." Being sincere means "being yourself." We tend to define growth and development by separation and individuation, by "cutting the apron strings" or "getting out on our own." We seem to believe that the goal of living is individual autonomy. While that may be an important, indeed a primary, task during certain stages of childhood, adolescence, and early adulthood in some cultures, it may not necessarily be the end point of all personal growth. The process of emerging from the womb into the arms and then the lap, the playpen, the yard, of going from the yard to the school, and of finally leaving home, is one of continuously increasing individuation. A central theme of our development from conception to the height of adolescence may be the search for identity, but it is not an absolute or irreversible goal.

Even at the height of self-discovery, other potentials are also active. Even proudly individualistic people must realize that existence and identity are largely dependent on past relationships. We begin to differentiate ourselves from the network of our early relationships primarily through a process of "introjection" and "internalization." That is, we bring into and make part of ourselves the behavior and emotional states of others. We are strong enough and brave enough to leave our parents' presence when we have internalized their voices and know what they would allow us to do. The entire complex of our consciousness develops largely by absorbing parts of meaningful people in our lives. We may experience our consciousness as the seat of our privacy, as personal and secret, and yet it is acquired and maintained through social interaction. As the few "feral" children who have survived alone in the wilds have taught us, without any normal social stimulation, without a model in the world about us, without intimate relationships, we would never develop a consciousness of "self," a definition of "I." We do not *become* the people from whom we learn anymore than we become the food we eat, but an aspect of them does become a part of us. As we need protein in our bodies, so we need a social-reference group in our minds.

But as important as the struggle for individuality is, and though such consciousness serves a useful function in the world, it is not necessary to assume that individuality is a stable or even a desirable state to maintain. In striving for uniqueness and separateness, we have a tendency to submerge or even ignore a parallel development in our consciousness which is continuous with our more diffuse origins—our earliest state of merged consciousness with the world and with others. For a century or more, psychologists have recognized that the infant's state of consciousness may hold a key to some of the more exotic psychological phenomena which invade everyday reality. In *Civilization and Its Discontents* Freud saw "early phases of ego-feeling" as the precedent of oceanic feelings described by many people. He suggested that "the origins of the religious attitude can be traced back in clear outlines as far as the feeling of infantile helplessness." Freud thus argued that the child is father to the man. For he viewed adult reactions and relationships as reflections of behaviors learned during the critical developmental periods of childhood.[1]

Many ecstatic traditions allude to fetal and infantile consciousness as the prototypes of spiritual bliss. A common metaphor for describing mystical experience is that of "rebirth." When we try to imagine what it was like to be an infant, we have to rely on our memories of ecstatic states, for we cannot be sure we are remembering our own infancy. In these ecstatic states, we are likely to experience a sense of merger or union with something outside our personal boundaries: God, the cosmos, nirvana. This is the reunifying experience of the adult. Rebirth in mystical experience is a metaphor and a reality, an attempt to regain a sense of wholeness, of merger, of being cared for that was our condition long ago.

For all their similarities, ecstatic experience is not simply the recapitulation of infantile experience. To say so would be to deny the importance of all experience beyond the toddler state in shaping our consciousness. Nor is it enough to equate the ecstatic state, as Jung did in his early writing, with the "thoughtless state of early childhood, where as yet no opposition disturbed the peaceful flow of dawning life, to which the inner longing always draws us back again and again." [2] Fetal and infantile consciousness are more than a provocative metaphor for future states of consciousness that are experienced as merger with something outside the "I." They are ecstatic experiences in their own right and furthermore they contain the origins of ecstatic consciousness. They are the prototypes of all future merger experiences but differ in basic ways from later ecstasies in that they take place in a pre-relational consciousness before the "I" has even evolved. Further, they are not one homogeneous epoch, but a series of states of consciousness, each of which is linked to a particular ecstatic orientation in the future, and whose over-all development will profoundly influence (though not limit) the form and meaning of our subsequent ecstatic development.

Infants move through four basic stages in the development of their consciousness before emerging with a sense of "I." From an initial stage of minimal differentiation, they gradually discriminate between those parts of the world which are part of their basic internal reality and those which are outside their being and neutral to their existence. At each stage they come closer to recognizing the boundaries of their own being and interacting with others as distinct persons. One who learns to recognize "I" learns to control relationships with "You."

The first pre-relational stage, the fetal experience, is conceptualized as a *merger with totality.* Psychologically undifferentiated from and physiologically fused with the mother, the fetus has no perception of personal boundaries or the limits of his being. He is literally at one with the world, a totally connected, dependent organism, virtually a sub-system of the mother, yet growing to an inner tune of his own. The boundaries between mother and fetus are regulated by a feedback so exquisite that from the beginning, separateness must be defined in terms of dependence. Such is the physiological reality of the pre-birth state. We can only guess at the psychological reflection of fetal existence, dominated as it is by an immature nervous system. Some psychological theorists believe that these experiences are "remembered" in non-verbal ways which later affect emotional patterns. Not surprisingly, "fetal consciousness" is one of the most frequent experiences in many mystical traditions. Some use the term as metaphor and others take it literally. The fetal position and fetal memory occur so often in adult life that it is difficult to ignore the possibility of trace memories, of subjective ties to our earliest experience.

Research findings have made the continuum between fetus and newborn existence more obvious. It is now known that for much of the pregnancy, there is electrical activity in the fetal brain. The fetus has rapid-eye-movement sleep (rem sleep) which in the adult is correlated with dreaming states. In fact, the ratio of "dream sleep" to non-dream sleep is much higher in the fetus. The expanding field of fetal neurophysiology strongly suggests that fetal consciousness precedes birth, at least if we broaden the definition of consciousness to include states more diverse than the simple waking state in which an awareness of the "I" is most predominant. We cannot deny fetal consciousness on the ground that we cannot remember it; if we were to discount all experience and events we cannot consciously recall, we would eliminate huge segments of our existence.

Pregnancy is rarely thought of as a relationship; it can easily be argued that neither party really knows or communicates with the other. One might also say the opposite, namely, that the knowledge and communication shared by these two beings, mother and child, will never again be as whole. In pregnancy, a profound relational consciousness (which some women have described in ecstatic terms) develops regardless of the lack of symmetry in its participants. Scientific and literary descriptions of pregnant women suggest that they indeed participate in a variety of altered states of consciousness in which their identity and their projections of the fetal identity are merged.[3] We cannot examine fetal consciousness in the same way that we can question the pregnant woman about her mental states; and thus it is inevitable that the pregnancy relationship is labelled as an inner state of the parent rather than as the physical and psychological merger of two beings. The fetus, whatever his consciousness, has no "point of view" since he has known no other reality. Perhaps the most important effect on him of his mother's experience during pregnancy is that she accepts the merger and allows her consciousness to reach out and expand to include his own; for the most practical aspect of their union occurs after they are physically separated but still paired in an extraordinary bond. Unless she can anticipate his needs as if they are her own, the infant may not physically survive or emotionally develop.

Birth does not create a sharp break in the mother/child relationship unless the two are separated through adoption or medical necessity. If they remain together as a social unit, they pass through an exquisite set of interrelated changes which reveal the extent to which the physiology of each is still dependent on the other. This is the physical counterpart to their psychological merger. It is not unusual, for example, for a mother to awaken to a cry that no one else in the household has heard. She may move her own mouth as she watches her infant suck; she may unconsciously assume an "*en face*" position, lining up her face with the infant's face and turning when he turns.[4] She may experience physical pain when he cries or have trouble breathing when her baby has a stuffy nose. When a new mother must leave her baby even for a few hours, she may feel an ache in her arms, or feel as though a part of her own body has been amputated. The first day or so after delivery, women may be particularly aware of the emptiness in their abdomen and the unaccustomed stillness within. Their milk may issue forth in a cycle exactly regulated to the feeding demands of the baby; and she may thus experience a sudden gush if she has left the baby home with a sitter. Even after the umbilical cord is cut, mother and child are linked in an extraordinary union which transcends the skin and space that are now between them.

In all intense relationships, the partners experience some sense of a shared subjectivity. We develop myths about identical twins and other pairs who feel each other's pain and recognize each other's dangers even when they are separated by great distances. We tell stories about men who vomit while their wives are pregnant and lovers who feel a pang when their beloved dies. We often turn to the para-psychological to explain the experiences of those who have lost someone close to them in death and are able to hear the voice of their loved one through a medium. It is difficult for us to discover that part of our beloved still within us after they die, for it is important to our cultural assumptions to maintain the illusion of ourselves as a separate "I." We fail to recognize the extent to which the "I" is lost in a close relationship, just as we place people in the special category of "mystic" if they lose their "I" in a cosmic experience. Our normal, sane social functioning seems to be premised on an assumption that "I" is "I" and "everybody else" is just that, every body, separate and inviolate.

Pregnancy and mother/infant relationships teach us that there is no need to search for unknown, para-psychological forces to explain how a mother hears an infant's cry or how someone experiences the emotions or thoughts of a dead brother or wife. For, experientially, we did not start our lives as separate entities. Each of us has struggled toward "I-ness" and individuality against the vague boundaries of our formless origins. Despite our physical separateness, when we emerge from the womb there is no "I" to confront the universe; rather we are a physiologically immature organism with enough reflex activity to sustain life only if a nurture system is devoted to our care. An infant lives as part of another, hearing another's voice as his or her own, feeling another's mannerisms, experiencing subtle grades of existence as conveyed by another's emotions. This is our original subjectivity. The potential and experience of merging with another is built into the psycho-biology of our earliest moments. With such beginnings, the wonder is that some of us are able to gain and partially maintain the subjective illusion of separateness.

Margaret Mahler, a pediatrician and psychoanalyst, has studied mother/infant and mother/toddler interactions in detail to discover how relationships develop. Her descriptions provide powerful evidence for the link between the development of infant consciousness and ecstatic experience. Mahler believes that the drama of birth is deceptive: "The biological birth of the human infant and the psychological birth of the individual are not coincidental in time. The former is a dramatic and readily observable, well circumscribed event; the latter a slowly unfolding intrapsychic process." [5] For Mahler, the psychological birth of the self is the process through which individual subjectivity is achieved. She calls this process "separation-individuation" and suggests that it is the dominant psychological task in the first three years of life, if not of the entire life cycle.

According to Mahler, the infant begins life without the concept of another person. He is in a state of "normal autism"; that is, he is not oriented toward the external environment, but rather perceives everything in a self-centered, omnipotent mode which Mahler describes as a "primitive hallucinatory disorientation." For the infant there are no boundaries, no identity, no inside or outside. There is only a universe of experience that *is*. The mother is the total world even though she is not yet perceived as a person apart from the rest of the things which surround him. He is totally fused with her nurturing system which envelops his experience and consciousness. Selma Freiberg describes the condition similarly:

> He can't be mad at his mother because he hasn't yet learned that there is a person outside of himself who satisfies his needs. He's not complaining to the management because he doesn't know that the management is responsible for his meal. He experiences hunger, and something is put into his mouth that brings satisfaction. If we can risk an analogy, his meal comes to him like those bottomless mugs and pitchers of the fairy tales, always brimming over with an intoxicating liquor, always magically on hand when need arises, or the magic syllable is uttered. And the disappointing truth is that at this stage he does not reflect upon the source of supply any more than you or I think about a utility company when we turn on a tap to get water or press a switch to bring light.
>
> . . .
>
> For these first weeks are not entirely a time of darkness and primeval chaos. An invisible web is spun around the child and his mother that emanates from the mother and through which the most subtle impressions are transmitted to the child. And while the infant doesn't "know" his mother, can't recognize her on sight, he is receiving an infinite number of impressions through physical contact with her that gradually lead to the formation of his image of her.[6]

Mahler refers to this remarkable relationship between mother and infant as "symbiotic." Mother and infant are functionally fused to their mutual advantage. The fusion is asymmetrical. The infant's actual survival rests on its continuance, while a new mother will continue to live if her infant dies, although she will suffer considerable psychological pain, indeed illness. For the infant, it is not the person of the mother that matters, but rather her functions. The mother's hypersensitivity to the infant's needs helps her perform this role. Her breasts, skin, arms, and comforting noises are marvellous providers for the first few months. The infant will not perceive the total person beyond these encompassing parts and functions. The individual is interchangeable with any other total system that would continue to provide the same comforting services—father, nanny, grandmother, or other surrogate.

While a surrogate may satisfy the infant perfectly well in the first few months, the same is not true for the mother. If the mother enters the nurturing role for her infant, she will continue to be involved in a relationship in which her personal boundaries are almost as completely blurred as they were during pregnancy. The infant has just emerged from the depths of her being. Her fantasies about the child, produced by her own psychological needs, have not yet been related to the infant's separateness. The mother is still profoundly connected to an unknown creature fashioned from her own projections.

The experiences of the mother and the infant are complementary. Neither truly perceives the other as a separate being. For the mother, there is a tiny creature whose dominant characteristic may be that he is "mine," virtually an appendage. For the infant, there is total selfless merger with a world of sensations that is still unformulated and amorphous. Together the mother and infant gradually emerge from their dreams and begin to assert themselves as individuals.

Sometime after the third month, the infant begins to display behavior suggesting a change in relation to the universe around him. He begins to perceive the world outside. If we observe his behavior closely, we may notice that he is changing his relationship to the universe, seeing some boundaries, realizing that care does not flow automatically. He does not yet know that he is a self merged with another. Rather there is an "us" and the outside. "Outside" means objects to look at, things to thrash toward, loud noises to complain about, faces to react to. Sometimes these things are so interesting that sucking can be forgotten. Even rocking may become an annoying distraction if there is a particularly delightful bauble to watch.

Once the infant begins to perceive the outside world, he has moved to the second stage of pre-relational consciousness, *merger in the dyad.* He and the mother are now a true "symbiotic" dyad. He begins to perceive boundaries of self, but these are vast and diffuse, definitely including the mother in the self-part rather than in the outside-part. We cannot be precise in our conceptual reconstruction of a period we do not recall. Neither can we be sure how and why the changes occur. But it is likely that they are developmental, that a maturing nervous system which encounters the typical infant's environment and experience gradually makes more and more differentiations. Mahler suggests that the motive for making an initial discrimination between the dyad and the outside world lies in the infant's awareness of the good, warm, secure experience consistent with his mother's presence and that of the bad, cold, insecure experience that occurs when his mother is not present.

This initial, rudimentary perception of self and non-self is perhaps a more dramatic change in the individual's development than physical birth. The infant's experience of merger has begun to shift from totality to a special person. This person may not yet be recognized or even acknowledged, but the first steps toward interpersonal relating have in fact been taken. The two halves of the dyad are beginning to recognize the specific source of their emotions, the human element in their experience. Merger with totality may be a pleasurable experience, an ecstatic state to which many adults would like to return, but it is too vague a realm for the infant to influence. When the "non-self" world is established, then a smile or a gesture of gratitude can be directed at the appreciated, pleasure-giving inside-self world. As the "self" environment surrounds the infant, he coos, smiles, gurgles in recognition and appreciation. The person who makes up this environment is pleased, flattered, and rewarded for her efforts.

The increasing discrimination within the dyad is continuous. There is no one day in which the infant suddenly recognizes that there are boundaries. He gradually makes increasingly refined discriminations within the dyad that he experiences as self. Sounds seem to occur in certain spaces within the union. Some movements apparently take place only when the whole "self" world is present. Others, along with certain bodily sensations, seem to occur even when the outside, the "other" environment is still predominating. The infant begins to perceive his own body and its functions as distinct from his mother's. Some things are his, irrespective of her, although she seems to have a profound influence on them. One noise will stop when she appears; another (gentler) one will start in her presence. Gradually, the "self" separates from the "non-self." The baby sees mother and begins to explore baby, discovering the wonder of the things he can influence and all that he can make happen. The more he can accomplish, the more the baby has emerged as a conscious, controlling entity. He must be developing an awareness of "self" and discriminating between the important parts of his "non-self" world as he begins to manipulate the environment and initiate complex interactions. His perception of the "non-self" world becomes more complicated, for in it there are neutral objects and intimate objects, plus that one special object who is the other half of the original dyad.

As the baby learns to assert his power and manipulate his environment, he confronts the origin of conflict in interpersonal relating. For the first time there can be intricate encounters between two separate selves. The two halves of the dyad begin to recognize each other as complicated and separate entities with distinct wishes and needs. They learn to accommodate each other as more than idealized projections.

During the period of the merged dyad, the mother and infant are accustomed to each other. They are operating on their own interrelated rhythms. They know their own shared smells and sounds and their own favorite ways of touching each other. They seem almost clairvoyant in their sensitivity to each other's needs and movements. They are fused. As the stage of dyadic symbiosis ends, the infant becomes increasingly aware of the mother as a separate entity, apart from himself, but also apart from the rest of the world. Mother is special; she is unquestionably recognized.

Mahler uses the recognition of mother by baby as the end of the total blending between infant and mother and the beginning of the separation and individuation of the infant from the mother. It is only the beginning, however. The child generally takes two more years to stabilize his sense of mother as a totally distinct and separate person, one he can happily walk away from even when he knows he may not see her again for hours. In practice, this process is never really complete. We all have a yearning for that period in our lives when we were warm and secure and merged with a powerful, protecting force. Few of us reach a point where we can perceive our own parents as simply people, as individuals with whom we should relate as equal adults in the mundane world. Parents retain some of the magic that they held for us when we were infants. We either believe they know our hidden thoughts and motives or feel resentment that they do not know them. The normal child separates himself first from totality, then from the dyad, but he never totally escapes the emotions that accompanied these stages.

Once the baby shows a definite preference for his mother, he is signalling an awareness of the two distinct parts of the dyad; the experience of total merger is behind him and even the dyadic union is diluted. He is now likely to recognize friends, enemies, and neutrals. He not only knows more about what is happening inside the dyad, he is also beginning to react more to people outside the dyad. He begins to alternate between kinds of relating. He can relate to himself, to the outside world, or to his mother. When he can crawl, he can choose to leave his mother, to explore other objects and people. He can develop special relationships with additional members of the family. He may seek out his brother or give a special smile to his father. He starts to incorporate other family members into his fleeting sense of "self." They are not part of the negative non-us any more.

Thus by six or seven months the infant is entering a third stage of pre-relational consciousness, *merger in the group*. His boundary is being stretched to include significant others outside of the mother/infant dyad. Faces and gestures of individuals are observed and touched as if to find out who qualifies for entrance into this first and most sacred club of "self." These new persons in the infant's life are checked against the face and gestures of the mother, now in wonderment and at other times in despair. As the criteria for election to this "club" are broadened to include familiar faces and gestures belonging to others besides those of the mother/child dyad, the concept of outside also becomes more specific. The "stranger reaction," an apprehensive, anxious, startled response in the child when confronted with an unfamiliar face, develops sometime after six months and before one year. It signals an entirely new complex level of perception. By this point, the symbiotic dyad has been replaced by an "inside," bounded "self" containing a mosaic of familiar persons. The outside "non-self" contains individuals and objects recognized as "not belonging."

It is difficult to imagine the subjective experience that corresponds to these developmental changes. The infant is no longer as totally filled up with the merged world of mother/infant. Other people have become part of that consciousness. The child's new sense of inside is probably closer to a blend of gestures and faces, some of which are more linked to his sense of self than others. The overwhelming sense of "mother/self" dissipates as the circle of accepting selves is enlarged and the dyad gives way to *group merger.* The primacy of the mother-child union in the child's world of "self" slowly gives way to a union with multiple others within the family environment. Dyadic consciousness crystallized out of the earlier state of merger with totality; it now gives way to group consciousness.

The kind of primitive self-consciousness sensed by the infant at this stage of development may be analogous to the adult's experience of ecstatic involvement in a group ceremony. Adults can become so immersed in the group entity that their "I-ness" is virtually lost. Their behavior is dictated by their role in the group and their thinking is experienced as part of the group mind.

Individuals caught up in such experiences, such as mobs, intense work groups, religious groups, athletic teams, and the like, perceive the non-group outside as alien. It readily becomes tinged with paranoiac hostility while the group inside becomes the "supra-consciousness." Individual identity is submerged in the group's independent life; the "I" becomes a fleeting, insignificant sensation. Participation in a group is an engrossing experience; the individual is literally lost in union with others.

The loss of "I" that is part of profound group experiences is tempered by an awareness of pressure by the group to conform and the loss of the "self's" ability to respond beyond the limits of the role dictated by the group. We may experience a conflict between whether to "go with the crowd" and allow further submergence of the "I" into the group consciousness, or whether to emerge from the "mass-self" as an individual. The obscurity that a group provides may be comfortably irresponsible. That same obscurity may also be a potent stimulus to search for an identity that will establish the "self" above and beyond the group. This is the force which creates charismatic leaders or dictators out of individuals who are particularly sensitive to prolonged loss of "self." Their "I" becomes the group; they need the group to feel whole.

The child of six to nine months old cannot yet experience this conflict between merging with the group and maintaining the "I." There is not yet a true individual identity. He is just beginning to develop a "self" boundary which encompasses more than the symbiotic dyad. This stage of primitive group consciousness, in which the "self" is experienced as a mosaic of the selves around him, furthers the separation from the original pair and heightens the embryonic individual identity. As the child experiences part of his own potential in each new piece of his mosaic "self," he begins to discover an "I" that is constant in all these situations.

For the child, this enlargement of "self" beyond the dyad increases the scope of his actions and makes him dependent on many other social configurations than the maternal relationship. Like any other role player, he explores the potentials of each new group situation. He may begin to play with other children, showing independence with them in ways that would be impossible if he were alone with his mother. A unique set of behavior develops when he is alone with his father or other parenting figures who were rather distant in earlier infancy, but who now become increasingly important. He may behave one way when alone with his father and another way when his mother is still in the room. He may "merge" in the family constellation without being as obviously tied to the mothering relationship but become "one of the kids," finding times and ways that he can be acknowledged, seeking his special place in the family society.

The infant's consciousness of "self-as-a-group" is an important developmental step toward an awareness of individuality and consciousness of the "I." The sense of merger in a group is probably less intense than the infant's "pre-self" union with totality or the dyad. Similarly, the adult's experience of ecstasy in a group is intense but often feels plastic and superficial when compared to dyadic love.

Out of the matrix of his "group self" the child of two gradually comes to perceive himself as a unique and separate person with an "I." He is entering a fourth stage of pre-relational consciousness, that of the "heightened I." He is continually in the flux of feeling separate, while powerfully supported by a potent biological push toward ever increasing independence and at the same time being part of a larger union. The child is learning to stand by himself, to recognize his name, to particularize his mastery of the universe through speech. The toddler discovers his power as an individual. He is like a god, recreating the world in his own image. There is enormous pleasure gained with each new skill. His consciousness of new identity transforms each encounter with the ordinary into a magical act. An erect little girl walks three steps across a floor shrieking with joy as she falls into her mother's arms. A proud little boy shouts "go away" toward a huge dog and stands in awe as the beast moves away. He beams and declares, "I did it, I did it," then turns to confront his family in his new and absolute strength. There is no end to the joyful power of this new individual as he conquers the world. And always there is the return to mother, to sister, to the family, where he can slip into "self-state" transcendence while being held or sucking on the ubiquitous blanket. He can retreat briefly from the pull of the magical "I."

Some psychologists have referred to this ego state as "the ideal state of self." [7] They speak of his "inflated sense of omnipotence . . . magical powers . . . as the result of his spurt in autonomous function." The mood is one of elation, mania, with a sense of total competence. Every action and perception is newly individualized, seen for the first time with an individual pair of eyes. In such a state of consciousness, there is a precarious balance between awe and fear. The ego is seen in terms of what can be done, how much achieved; the more diffuse, merged state of consciousness is relegated to a shadow world, a faint memory, that seems to re-emerge only in moments of regression. Yet the euphoric magic relies heavily on the subjective reality of merger to cover the fragile beginning of individuality, the naked, small, and helpless individual who must now encounter the frightening and unyielding world of people and things.

The state of a heightened "I" is the archetype of an achievement-oriented person addicted to production, growth, and individualism. It would be suitable for any Horatio Alger story, for there are no limits on ability and enthusiasm. This has been the ideal of our culture, which is why our psychologists have seen it as the "ideal state of self." Perhaps less individualistic cultures would see it differently. For some people the change from a merged and symbiotic identity to the heightened "I" is maladaptive and experienced as a loss of the preferred realm, not as a positive accomplishment.

Under the press of overproduction and overpopulation, our

society seems to be moving away from its emphasis on individual achievement toward more support of community and group-living skills. Child-rearing has begun to reflect this shift in values. We may see a change in the way that the shift from group to individual consciousness is handled in our children. Cultural supports and maternal attitudes may change the toddler's emerging individuality from successful accomplishment to failure. A mother with a profound need to share her consciousness with her infant can be puzzled by the emergent personality characteristics which do not fit into her fantasies, into her ideal projection of her child. Other mothers are threatened by the dyadic phase and eager to give up the invasive presence that enveloped their consciousness. Similarly, fathers and siblings may either welcome the change from one stage to another or experience it as new competition in their own lives. Whatever the special reactions in the environment of each particular child, the entire family equilibrium must shift to accommodate the unique consciousness that now insistently demands recognition as an "I."

It is the world of relationships that is most affected by the individual's emergence from the earlier states of merger. Previously, the child could be taken for granted, merging and becoming part of others instead of interacting with them or making demands on them. Once the child recognizes separateness, others are treated in an entirely new way. They may be disobeyed, contradicted, or refused. The toddler asserts independence. Such confidence may become a physical danger until it is accompanied by judgment and cooperation. This is the time of the "terrible two's," when active and curious children swallow poison, roll off porches, and jump confidently from trees. Each child forces the world to notice him. Others may not take him for granted.

The child is probably the last to become aware of the change in the way important people relate to him. There is almost always a look of surprise and shock when he is told not to do something. He can have a temper tantrum when his concept of his own potency is firmly challenged. The sweet achievement of separateness has not yet been tempered by the enormity of what he has lost. When others impose limits, they establish an awareness of the separation, the price paid for individuality.

The awareness of separateness and uniqueness allows reality-based relationships for the first time. Previously, other people were not actually encountered except as part of the child's own subjective world. The infant's form of knowing was not based on interaction and feedback. Others were known (if such a term can be used) as part of one's identity rather than as separate in themselves. As the "I" grows in strength, the mystical union with totality, the sense of being a part of a larger unit, the primordial merger between mother and infant, or between family group and child, fades into a fantasy which will become the germinating seed of a variety of ecstatic quests.

The more the "I" is known, the more important relationships become. The *unawareness* of being enclosed in a comforting emotional blanket develops into an *awareness* of being alone and apart from others. And with that separateness comes melancholy, insecurity, and the desperate urge to find someone in a relationship who can satisfy a lingering hunger for a more profound intimacy.

For the first time, the child must learn skills to recapture love and warmth. It is a terribly difficult task for which there is little preparation. Happily for most children, separation and identity are achieved gradually. Mother and family are there to blend with when needed. The relational skills that evoke security and comfort are minimal at the beginning. Nevertheless, the discovery of "you" and "other," unlike the joyous discovery of the "I," is fraught with anxiety. The elation of the early toddler may give way to dependence, helplessness, and whining. The mother is wooed, sought after, relied upon, in dramatic contrast to the mindless independence that had earlier been the child's style. Now he clings and wants more from a mother who is busy doing other things.

The child who has learned to know his name and take pride in the smallest self-accomplishment must begin to win back what he has lost, using an entirely different set of rules. It is truly a fall from mystical grace for the sake of self-knowledge.

Learning how to relate to others is a lifetime task. With each new biological or social development in the life cycle, new difficulties arise and new skills must be acquired. At each stage there are new potentials for ecstasy, new opportunities for merger, but complications at the mundane level of relating are also new and must be overcome. There is always a new game to be played and the possibility that a player may win a few moments of profound interaction or intense emotion. Behind all the skills, games, masks, and scripts which we use both to ward off intimacy and become close to people, there is a glimmer of another reality. Behind each bit of social repartee and custom is the possibility of more, an echo of that time when there was no need for confrontation and interaction but only existence and merger. Adults develop patterns for evoking ecstatic experience, techniques for returning to the world of union and merger.

Some adults are oriented toward totality. For them ecstatic sex is cosmic sex; the object is universal myth rather than a person or even the genitals. Drug ecstasies move toward fusion with nature or the universal deity and religious experience toward involvement with an all-encompassing religious system. Love is idolatry and idealization, the partner expanded to godhood. These adults strive for an experience patterned on their earliest infantile state of merger with totality.

Other adults are oriented toward the dyad. Sex, drugs, and religion are all-transcendent enhancers of the experience of ecstatic dyadic merger, or in other words, love. They search for a world consisting of a single Other; and they desire to live with a sense of being united with a caring partner who shared their most intimate rhythms and makes their sense of self an expanded, dyadic awareness.

Yet other adults are oriented toward the group. For them

ecstatic sex is group sex, either through fantasy, ritual orgy, or its modern counterparts. Drugs are best in a group context; the commune, ceremonial, or rock festival provides the ultimate "turn on." Their religious experience takes place at mass evangelical gatherings or encounter groups. Their love affairs are with social causes and nationalistic movements. They strive toward an ecstatic state in which they are part of a network of selves functioning as a single merged entity.

Other individuals prefer to experience a heightened "I," a feeling of intensified personhood. Sex is masturbation whether the partner is present or not. Drugs and religious experience are ego trips whose theme is personal power. Love is of one's body, one's person, one's individual development. The elation of heightened awareness is exhilarating, but the ecstatic state of true merger and loss of "I" in group, dyad, or totality may be perceived as negative or frightening.

The induction of ecstatic states almost always begins with the development of a heightened "I" in which, like the toddler, we are caught up in a powerful awareness of our body, our movements, our accomplishments, and our attachments to the world. To progress further into ecstatic consciousness we divest ourselves of individuality, lose our awareness of boundaries and objects, and experience merger with our environment.

Group and dyadic merger sometimes become vehicles of a sense of merger with totality. The individual first experiences union with the group or the Other and then moves into an experience of merger with totality. This progression is visually represented in elaborate mandalas which depict a progression of multiple god forms leading through ecstatic pairs until the ultimate harmony is portrayed at the center as the godhead (perhaps an abstract symbol). The "blank-out" experience in which the end result of frenzied dancing is total obliteration, loss of memory, or even unconsciousness may be an experience of group performance which leads through a sense of union with the group to an experience of union with totality. Thus sex too can be experienced as universal oneness rather than dyadic union.

For most of us the boundaries between orientations are not rigid. We may enjoy all kinds of settings, whether in isolation, in pairs, or in a group. And yet we may also consistently seek out one or the other for our peak experiences. We learn that solitary walks on the beach at sunset are more enriching for us than romance or partying; or that psychedelic drugs, prayer, or sex is better shared with a single Other rather than in isolation or with many others. We gravitate to a particular form of ecstatic experience because it feels better suited to who we are.

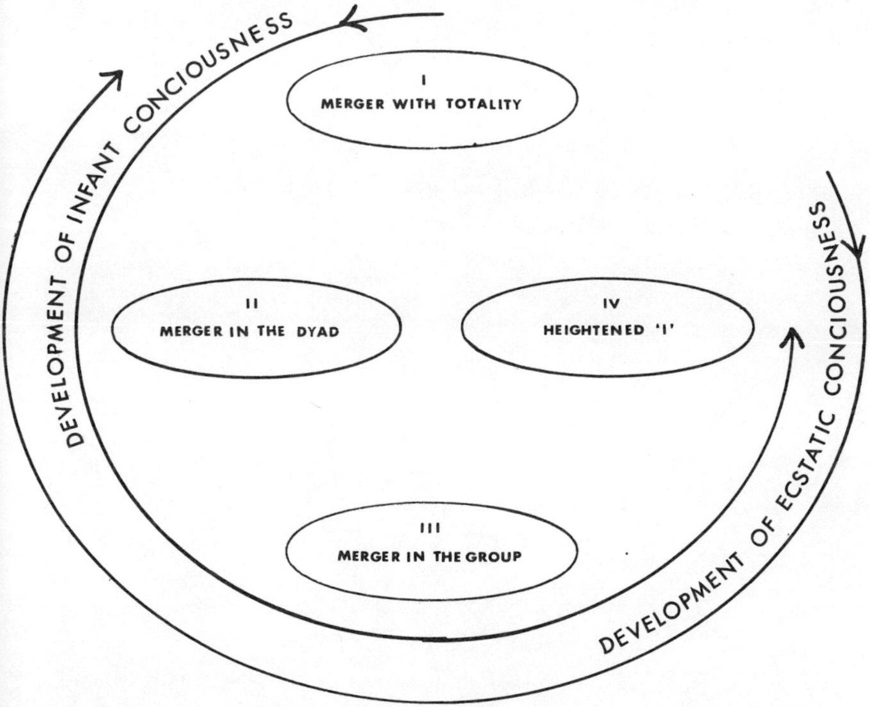

The infant's experiences as he moves through each pre-relational merger state influence his tendency to seek out a particular kind of ecstatic experience in later years. In general, the influence of early developmental factors on subsequent behavior is complex and subtle. Presumably, the same is true of ecstatic experience.

An extended dyadic merger state in infancy might provide a desirable model for future love experiences; or it might drive the young child away from a smothering dyadic relationship into seeking more solitary or group modes as he develops. The lack of supportive mothering and family life may prod a child to look for ecstatic experience in solitary ways; or it might leave him with an enormous longing for merger with one Other or with a group. No exact blueprint is possible here, only the likelihood that three years of pre-relational consciousness provide the crucial framework for ecstatic life and ecstatic orientation in the future.

5

The Development of Ecstatic Relationships in Childhood

INFANTS are described as being in a *pre-relational* stage because they have not yet developed a consciousness of their unique being, separate from totality, the Other, or the group. They have not yet developed a sense of being in relation to another, although they have strong attachments and meaningful interactions. As infants progress through the various stages of merger, an "I" gradually crystallizes out from the more diffuse origins of consciousness. Children of three are heir to this process. Their future development will be increasingly labelled as a search for identity. Each step toward greater individuality will be marked by greater facility for adaptation in day-to-day "reality." By adulthood, individual identity is almost a fixed notion. Ecstatic merger experiences may be walled off from day-to-day existence, except for the few who choose to devote their lives to such a pursuit.

The universality of ecstatic experience strongly suggests that we cannot leave our pre-relational origins behind us even when we have developed our identity and are relating fully with others. The potential and the form of merger experience are carried with us even as we continue to establish the boundaries between "I" and the world outside. As it is difficult to integrate these two disparate experiences of the world, we therefore all have a developmental tendency to submerge one at the expense of the other. Children feel the tension between separateness and union more acutely than adults, for the world of subjective merger states is still very immediate to them. They spend a great deal of energy trying to reconcile the reality just being organized by their emerging individuality with the other reality that up until now has dominated their consciousness. It is possible to understand a great deal about childhood development by tracing the transformations of this conflict between merger and individuation.

When children emerge from the pre-relational state in which various forms of merger have dominated their consciousness, they are faced with the overwhelming task of forming relationships on their own. They may be struggling to maintain their heightened sense of "I" and desperate to avoid dependence on those who threaten to overpower them, yet they must confront another individual without becoming lost and overwhelmed. They must work to acquire skills in relating.

Family interactions are demanding and complex. For the three year old, they are necessary but at times unwanted. Children often use the privacy of a quiet, secret place to retreat into themselves and seek out other states of consciousness. They discover ways to induce ecstatic feelings unrelated to merger with another person. Perhaps they return to their earliest feelings, now associated with objects or settings rather than mother, by touching a blanket, rubbing a bottle, or fondling a toy. They may repeat a magic formula over and over, stare at a single object, or enter a fantasy world in which they identify with a bird, cloud, or fictional character, to escape the demands of reality and of relating. These flights are away from relationships, away from confrontations and conflicts, away from struggles they are having with the important people in their lives for independence in the face of simultaneous needs for dependence. Retreating starts early in childhood, but the theme of trying to escape from relationships into a personal trance state continues throughout life. In *The*

Silver Crown, a children's book by Robert C. O'Brien, the heroine wakes up on her tenth birthday to discover a silver crown on her pillow. That very day her entire family and her home are destroyed. She finds herself alone with the crown, which turns out to be magic:

> She could feel the glow of the stones . . . pass through her head . . . she had a feeling of serenity and strength . . . the sunlight on the wall was a stained glass window . . . faint music, a hushed, sustained chord sung by a far-off choir . . .[1]

Every fairy tale about a child who gets lost in an enchanted forest carries in it this dream to escape briefly from the family into a world of solitary ecstasy.

Very young children may try to act *in relation to* others outside of the family, who are people with whom they have never been fused and whom they can confront more objectively. A normal two and a half year old who has no skills for playing *with* another child will play next to others. Educators call this phenomenon "parallel play"; it can be observed in any park sandbox. Two little ones will sit fairly near each other and make remarkably similar gestures, playing the same games, digging, pouring sand over their own legs, glancing at each other from time to time, but never actually speaking or interacting. They gain satisfaction merely from the presence of the other. Older children react with contempt and resentment toward the copycat, yet a three-year-old girl is expressing profound respect and attachment when she mimicks the moves and interests of another girl. She needs this model more than a beauty queen needs a mirror; for in it she discovers her own potentials, her own being, her own boundaries. Three year olds may still get confused from time to time, like the little boy who cries and insists on being kissed whenever his brother gets hurt, genuinely believing he received the bruise himself.

Sometimes it is difficult for a child to move into the stage of interactive play with other children. Some want so badly to communicate but are so lacking in skills that they hit, kick, or shove when they really want to say, "Will you play with me?" It is not unusual for a three year old to take someone else's place or steal his toy when he feels a need to interact with that other. Among any group of pre-schoolers, the phrase "Hey, I was using that first" will come up as one child responds to an overwhelming internal pressure to become the other child by performing his movements and possessing his things. Sometimes children discover how to use cultural archetypes to overcome the difficulties of relating as real people; two little boys who squabble over their toys may start calling each other Batman and Robin and suddenly acquire a whole new set of rules for how to relate toward each other without conflict. Young children do not initiate relationships easily. They must constantly fight the powerful urge to merge through primitive imitation or possession.

Even while children are beginning the struggle for status, for their own relationships, and discovering ecstasy in new realms, alone and outside their homes, they may retain enough basic trust in and feeling of security among the members of their families to experience a loss of their own boundaries and the joy of union. The potential for merger is there: it happens in an overwhelmingly warm hug or at night when they snuggle into their covers and are kissed by parents who come to tuck them in. Unexpected moments of merger with members of their family continue as their fundamental love experience.

Love relationships can begin as soon as children know their own uniqueness and the uniqueness of the Other; when they are no longer merged identities and thus stand *in relation to* another; when they add an awareness of "I" to their developing "self." The paradox for all of us, both as child and adult, is that *in order to experience ecstatic feelings in a relationship, part of us must return to the fusion state out of which our identity has been forged, while the rest of us exercises our skill at relating.* Children of three or four love when they subjectively co-exist in the two planes of relational reality: the earliest merger state and the later interactive state. At first, because the pre-relational past is so soon behind them, there is a continuous flow between these states, like the flickering in and out of consciousness that characterizes the entry and re-entry stages of mystical experience. But the developmental push is toward ever increasing separateness, which demands ever improved interactive skills. The child's individual boundaries harden. He begins to learn how to compartmentalize his ecstatic feelings in his dealings with people.

Learning how to get along often takes children in the opposite direction from their experience of profound pleasures. Ecstatic feelings may continue to be experienced with mother, father, and siblings, but they are less frequent and more difficult to maintain. Private ecstasies, on the other hand, are more within the emerging individual's control. They become increasingly important. A frightened two year old clings to her mommy; an anxious four year old is more likely to clutch his penis or put his finger in his mouth.

Nevertheless, ask a child about love, about the feeling he has with someone he really likes, and the response will be intense. At first the question may have little meaning for him until he gets in touch with his feelings and overcomes his fear of the regressive pull they exert. One four year old said that for him love was "like a window breaking inside my head." He became suddenly intense as he experienced the sensation. He said it was like "red and green and white all mixed together." And here he began to gesture wildly with his hands until he hugged his mother passionately. An older child, aged seven, began her answer by identifying the people she loved best, which included all the members of her family plus her dog. She said that "love was liking someone very, very much." Then she added in more emotional tones another "very much." She went on describing love as "respecting and trusting someone, someone you can count on trusting *inside.*" When asked where she felt love, she pointed to her heart, then enlarged the area to her entire chest.

"Sometimes when I really love someone like Mom or Dad, I feel it in my head too, and then, Wow!" At this point the child showed an expression of intense pleasure. "You feel you really love them. It's unbelievable!" Anyone observing children respond to such a question will have little doubt that they experience love as ecstasy in the context of a relationship.

It seems absurd to have to argue that children experience love. It is self-evident to those who raise, educate, and play with children that they are capable of the most intense feelings toward others that would be called love at more verbal stages in the life cycle. And yet almost all psychologists who have written about love believe that children under ten are incapable of loving at all. Thus Erich Fromm writes in *The Art of Loving*:

> For most children before the age from eight and a half to ten the problem is almost exclusively that of *being loved*—of being loved for what one is. The child up to this age does not yet love; he responds gratefully, joyfully to being loved. At this point of the child's development a new factor enters into the picture: that of a new feeling of producing love by one's own activity. For the first time, the child thinks of giving something to mother (or to father), of producing something—a poem, a drawing, or whatever it may be. For the first time in the child's life, the idea of love is transformed from being loved into loving, into creating love.[2]

Fromm makes the distinction clear in the form of an epigram: "Infantile love follows the principle, 'I love because I am loved.' Mature love follows the principle, 'I am loved because I love.' " We have all seen young children who apparently spontaneously present their mother with a special work of art, come home with a dandelion for their father, or insist on buying a new collar for their dog's birthday. Fromm would say that such a child was impelled by need rather than by feelings about giving. "Immature love says, 'I love you because I need you.' Mature love says, 'I need you because I love you.' "

Fromm has derived his theory of love from Sullivan, who has

written that "when the satisfaction or security of another person becomes as significant to one as one's own satisfaction or security, then the state of love exists." [3] This is a beautiful description of one kind of relationship. Like the golden rule, it is an idealized goal, a definition of social maturity. But it reserves love for an elite who are developing toward that particular kind of adaptation. By concentrating on the relational part of love, it leaves out the experience of ecstasy. It puts satisfaction and security before the overwhelming feeling of what is happening between two people becoming one. It excludes child love, adolescent love, homosexual love—in short, all forms of love which do not rest on socially defined "mature" relationships. It states an ideal without incorporating the process and the experience of being in love.

Relationships change during the life cycle and so therefore does the love experience. A child's relationships may be "immature." To a young person, maturity may be synonymous with whatever is stifling and staid. It may seem like a quality which would take away the abandon and delight of the love experience. Child love is different from, but no less than, adolescent or parental love. In fact, the conditions for ecstatic relationships may well be at their height at the very moment when individuality and separation are just beginning. As long as the child is able to trust the people in his environment enough that he is willing to return to remembered states of fusion with another, he is capable of loving—even if his interactions are as dependent and selfish as Fromm and Sullivan suggest.

When the child emerges from his symbiotic state, he may be able to work on his developing identity and continue to see the people around him as his main source of pleasure. However, he may soon become afraid to regress to earlier fused states because it appears to be a loss of control or weakness. Simultaneously, he has to work harder for attention and approval. He begins to realize that he has been taken care of by people who can forget or reject him from time to time. When he was in a merged state, emotional security seemed out of his control. Now he sees that it can be wooed. The newly emerged "I" feels vulnerable. He searches actively for pleasure and control, but simultaneously he yearns for dependence and security. He tends to establish two distinct kinds of relationships, one based on his dependency needs and the other on his desire for ecstasy.

The greatest psychological danger of the pre-relational years is that security (or, in Erik Erikson's term, basic trust[4]) may not be established. The child whose identity *is* the world, the dyad, or the group is incredibly sensitive to each real or threatened loss. It is literally a part of himself that is being ripped away and his inexperienced mind has no recourse to personal fantasy or a private world. The emergence of the "I" provides a possibility of choice about relationships and gives some protection from the extensive pain of loss. "I" may choose not to get involved, or to maintain a space between himself and others, or allow "them" to take care of him without feeling merged with "their" being. The choice is not conscious in an infant—it is learned from experience and need.

At each stage of development, the capacity for ecstasy in a relationship can be dulled or subverted. The earliest symbiotic attachment can be broken by a mother who is not able to develop the kind of sensitivity which allows for the merging of selves. If the child is forced to live through the turmoil and panic of inconstancy, he may lack the core sense of belonging which is the residue of the symbiotic experience. Another child may be pushed into becoming an individual, "a little man," by parents frightened by their own loss of identity at the pre-relational level or eager for performance and accomplishment from their offspring. These patterns may create children who need to reduce the pleasurable or merger aspects of a relationship in favor of a compulsive and stereotyped search for security. Even a family committed to ecstatic experience may move against close attachments by rewarding individual sensitivity and performance rather than relationships. It is virtually impossible to sort out which factors will lead a child to continue to strive actively toward ecstasy in relationships. The biological push toward independence assures development of movement, language, and cognition, all of which enhance relational skills, but they do not necessarily facilitate merger with another individual. When both trust and individuality have been well established, a child may dare to love.

The impetus to explore and master the universe may make a child resist being hugged and held. He may get greater and more reliable joy from manipulating cars, trucks, or dolls. Toys are replaceable; even a special blanket is replaceable when compared to the arms of a parent. And when a family member tries too hard to remain in profound contact with the child, the latter may be forced further and further from relationships which he knows from experience can be oppressive and demanding. When an adult has a pronounced need to remain in symbiotic relationship, the child does not develop a heightened capacity for symbiotic relating. Quite the contrary, when separation does not proceed normally, the child becomes unusually absorbed with himself and his fantasies. As a result he never gains a sensitive appreciation of others.

For love to occur in childhood, as in all other stages of life, the dual reality of relationship, interaction and fusion, must be experienced. The past is a guide but does not determine the kinds of relationship to be sought. The older the child becomes, the more he will choose for himself the object of his own ecstatic potential. Security, trust, relational skill, adequate separation, and continuing opportunities for fusion may all combine to provide a likely background for love to develop. But the conditions allowing for love are not the experience itself and their absence does not necessarily destroy the potential for love. The yoga master may feel secure, but he chooses to take the road to bliss alone. A sensitive, creative child may not search for a "stab of joy" in the world of relationships but may turn to dance or daydreams for her special ecstasy. On the other hand, an insecure child, dominated by her own need for security and comfort, may glimpse the mystic essence beyond dependence and learn to experience and search for her ecstasy in her relationships with people.

Dependency and ecstasy are two poles ordering the way in which relationships develop. In times of crisis, a moment of anxiety, loss, frustration, or simply the transient discontinuity of a new stage in development, the physical and emotional vulnerability of the child comes into sharp focus. Security and survival supersede all other needs. Any threat to budding individuality will increase a reliance on dependent relationships. Ecstasy must wait for a time when loss of identity can be experienced with joy, not anxiety; when dependency is a comfort, not a threat.

The child's tendency to resort to dependent rather than ecstatic relationshps in times of stress parallels society's tendency for baseline requirements for work, food, and shelter to supersede its commitment to the creative arts. The potential for pleasure is not eradicated but only submerged. Rats will starve themselves to death in order to continue to receive pure pleasurable stimulation in their midbrain. Devoted mystics will reduce their food intake to almost nothing if they believe that such a step is necessary to aid in the experience of nirvana. The quest for ecstasy will prevail no matter what conditions or penalties are exacted. But most of us when threatened will exaggerate that part of our important relationships which protect us. We will seek ecstasy in places that do not threaten the relationship. A married man or woman will seek out an affair with a new partner rather than experiment sexually with his or her spouse and risk throwing the old pattern off balance.

The ongoing conflict between dependency and ecstasy in a relationship is heightened by the development of more focussed sexuality in children. For newborns the entire body may be like an undifferentiated sensory receptor feeding potential pleasure into the brain. As they become more sensitive to the quality and intensity of each area, children recognize the peculiarly intense sensations associated with the orifices—the mouth, anus, and genitals. Infants who spend much of their time sucking on fingers, bottles, or blankets develop into children who seem always to be stroking their anus, penis, or vagina.

The psychoanalytical theory of personality rests on this assumption of infantile "sexuality," that is, on infantile awareness of the body's intense sensuality. For each child, conflicts arise between seeking the pleasurable sensations of the body (the physical paths to ecstasy) and accomplishing the psychological tasks associated with each stage of life. In general, psychological development rests on the child's ability to give up pleasure in order to gain control over his body, his relationships, and his environment. For example, bowel training rests on the ability of the child to give up the pleasurable freedom of doing what he wants when and where he pleases. He learns the more rigid, time-space control of toilet training. The mother and the rest of the family use displeasure or approval to pressure him toward increased control as his physical development makes each task possible. There are very few children capable of resisting, for they fear the threat to the dependency relationship. They would rather lose bodily pleasure than lose their relationship with the family.

It is difficult for most adults to admit to an association of ecstatic pleasure with bowel functions because our training for control and against pleasure in this area has been so extremely successful. Even when the anus is incorporated into a sexual repertoire it may carry with it disturbing psychological implications. We may have a distant memory of a voice telling us what is and what is not appropriate for that part of the body. The public was astounded by Marlon Brando in *The Last Tango in Paris* because he used anal sex, although his eroticism was rooted in punishment and pain rather than pleasure. The author of *The Sensuous Woman* recommends incorporating the anus into sexual activity, but admonishes her readers to be excruciatingly careful about washing the area carefully lest one repulse the partner. As children we may have experienced intense pleasure from the anal region, but for most of us these feelings have been driven deeply underground by the need to retain the security and comfort of our dependent relationship with our family.

Anal pleasures have generally been disassociated from relationships. Genital pleasures, on the other hand, are incorporated into adult relationships. Sex is a fairly reliable form of bliss. All our other pleasures, from opium to music, are saturated with sexual metaphors. Humans stimulated in the septal and nearby areas of their brains describe the resulting sensation as akin to orgasm or sexual excitement. We think of all really intense delights as sexual and yet regard sex as an adult pleasure. Thus we identify the beginning of the capacity to love with the blossoming of sexual maturity despite obvious evidence that children enjoy playing with their genitals and exploring the genitals of others. We forget how important sex was to us as children because we fought so hard to overcome our urges when striving to please the people we needed.

If we do have a "joy stick" akin to the lever that triggers brain stimulation for the rat, it is probably our penis or clitoris. From the moment children discover their genitals, they will stroke them pleasurably whenever they get the chance. Even the most liberal parents are disturbed by a child who masturbates perpetually. Therefore, children learn more surreptitious techniques. The child of three or four may suck his finger or blanket while being held in his mother's arms, using the mouth as a substitute for the preferred orifice because Mommy allows it. He is experiencing intense pleasure from his body and through his body while relating with his mother. He is becoming part of another person much as sexual lovers experience merger during intercourse. A little boy can rub his erect penis against his mother's body; a little girl can "ride a cock horse" on her father's leg. The children know they are getting intense, specific stimulation, but they learn that the grown-ups are more comfortable pretending that there is another kind of game going on. When the children are more direct and masturbate openly or ask to have their genitals stimulated, they are usually quickly distracted, pushed away, or punished by the guilty, frightened, or perhaps sexually aroused parent.

The ancient myth of Oedipus now names the remarkable period in child development when the sensations of the penis and vagina become openly intertwined with the love relationships in the family. It has been suggested that between the ages of three and five the genitals become more acutely sensitive to pleasure than they had been in infancy. Actually, children much younger than three may be passionately involved with their sex organs if they have access to them. Delightful gurgles accompany diaper changes when the genitals are bathed and stroked. In our society, diapers act as a combination codpiece and chastity belt before the age of three. Only with the end of bowel training are the penis and vagina really available to the child. Even more important, the family develops a new awareness of the child as an individual at about this time. With individuality comes a more active search for pleasure. They begin to make inner choices about the people around them. They choose their favorites for new reasons and may turn away from the one who has been taking care of their creature functions. A son may reject his dependent love of mother and seek an ecstatic relationship with his father. A once obedient and pliant daughter may boisterously initiate intimate encounters with her mother which exclude others, in particular her father. This is the stuff of jealousy and classic romantic triangles, for now children increasingly turn to those who give them most joy and draw their favorites away from others. It is no longer enough for them just to be taken care of anymore.

The Oedipus myth suggests that the son who kills his father and marries his mother will be permanently dishonored and rendered impotent. The child recognizes his romantic feelings and senses his father's jealousy. He strives to give up his sexualized desires because he does not want to risk the vengeance of the wronged parent. A similar dynamic affects the daughter, who is attracted to her father but fears competition from her mother. The Oedipal conflict is generally resolved by identifying with the parent of the same sex. By assuming the identify of his father, the male child is allowed to enjoy his mother; and vice versa. There are, of course, other solutions which range over the full spectrum of the variety of love choices. The way this developmental stage is handled by children has an extraordinary prophetic power over subsequent love relationships. That is why therapists explore adult adjustment in terms of childhood recollections. The defensive structures developed as variations, distortions, and displacements of primary loves persist and powerfully influence an individual's response to adolescent crush, first affair, marriage, later affairs, loss, and grief. It is as if these initial love relationships produce a mold upon which all subsequent loves are cast. When the form is altered, it is because the initial model has been reacted against or built upon, not because a new mold has been created. *As the initial merger states of the infant form the roots of ecstatic experience, so initial intense relationships in the Oedipal period project the future forms for ecstatic relationships.*

Oedipal theory is based on an adult viewpoint, on Oedipus already punished rather than lusting. This perspective is derived from analyzing what has happened rather than what is happening. If it emphasizes product rather than process, then no wonder love is viewed as a commodity reserved for mature adults. We have forgotten the marvellous bodily pleasure provided by the penis and vagina in our early years. But those first romantic relationships bore no tangible fruit. The child did not remain attached to his parents; he did not keep them as the objects of his lust. Therefore we tend to believe that he did not really "love" them.

In the developmental process, the intensity of the Oedipal love experience is what forces the reality of it to diminish. As the ecstatic attachment between mother and son and father and daughter progresses, the child probably realizes that genital attachment seems to have further consequences that he can only sense. Furthermore, the parent's adult lover is a dangerous rival who not only knows how to satisfy all levels of the parent's love, but also could destroy the child or refuse to take care of him.

Oedipal theory emphasizes the negative or punishing consequences of the child's lust and stresses the need for him to overcome this "problem" in his life. Thus the theory detracts from another level of reality for the child, namely, the actual ongoing love relationships in his life. The child of five cannot really have sex with his parents and would no doubt be frightened if this were somehow achieved. But he does experience intense love relationships. *Oedipal love contains the seed of all future love, but it is also a present love.* Its asymmetry makes it seem more transient and unreal than the love of "equals," but like all other loves it is problematic, tortuous, tumultuous. It survives with difficulty; at best it is continually changing to survive the developmental flux of the life cycle, the changing biological and social needs that are a part of growth and relationships at all ages. It should not be labelled childish or "cute," for that is to denigrate the characteristics of all love relationships, with which it shares the essential feature of ecstatic merger.

Children of five try very hard to learn how to relate on the most pragmatic and mundane levels. Their place in the family depends on their ability to learn ordinary social skills, not to enhance transcendent ones. If a son feels competition with his siblings or father for his mother's affection, the solution lies in out-manipulating his rivals rather than in continuing his passionate romance. The demands increase rather than decrease with success, for expectations rise. This is the day-to-day world of non-ecstatic relating which has emerged since separation of the "I" from prior merged identities.

But the other level of a relationship, the transcendent world of merged consciousness, in which "I" is an illusion and the other is still part of the self, is not completely buried. The child of five is still close to the time when all pleasure took place in merger with another. The pleasures of ordinary social interaction may seem safe but at the same time dull compared to a faintly remembered symbiotic relationship.

Romantic Oedipal relationships occur when children have a

magical perception of reality. As they gain a wider range of experience and increased competencies, they comprehend greater complexities and subtleties in reality but seek to hold on to magic through mythic perceptions. Children perceive the world in fairy-tale terms. They witness the procession of powerful kings and queens, miraculous transformations, magical events. A little girl's romantic feelings toward her father exalt him into an omnipotent, exquisite being in her day-to-day experience. It is easy for her to imagine his subjects quaking at every word. The hard part is to see him as a plain man and to recognize herself as a powerless little girl rather than as a princess or seductress. It is the social skills and identities that seem unattainable to the child. The mythic, ecstatic parts of a relationship are not yet hidden by social masks. The little girl finds it easy to believe that the prince really will come with that glass slipper, too small for the other women in the kingdom, and that she will shine forth, recognized for her effortless grace and beauty. It is harder to accept the dull reality that if she really wants recognition, she has to start making her bed, doing the dishes, or bringing home a good report card.

Children move away from formless, oceanic merger of the infant to more specific, visionary identification that may be complete with cast of characters and plot. The Tarot figures, the demi-gods of religions, the prophets, the cosmic players, the archetypal personages that are part of all ecstatic experiences embody children's projections about beings and relationships. Their movement toward more definition of the "I" has focussed and bounded ecstatic visions. Self and relationship are transformed into abstract patterns; and yet the pattern of an identity persists. The mythic vision is a layer interposed between "I" and merger on the road toward the ecstatic state. It is an attempt to control real relationships and hold on to magic and clarity, to ward off the confusion of secular reality.

This change in ecstatic mode from undifferentiated to particular is part of the same process of identity formation that has changed the selfless, fluid infant into an assertive, willful being.

Bodily pleasures too are now more specific; erotic areas can be deliberately exploited. Children can consciously choose the time, place, and relationship for experiencing the most profound pleasures. The chosen styles of pleasure (inside or outside of relationships) begin to have special meaning in relation to the new identity.

Bodily pleasures are closely associated with the formation of sexual identity. The child is labelled as a boy or a girl and all behavior, including ecstatic experience and love relationships, are ordered by these biological roles. The son learns to flirt with his mother, the daughter with her father, while learning to hold back slightly when they feel bodily pleasure in their relationship with the same-sexed parent. The child learns which side of the bed to crawl into, how to kiss each parent, and which genitals to express a desire for. Every relationship is affected by sexual roles. The unlimited panorama of love becomes limited by what is "appropriate" for age and sex. The child still scans the horizon for mythic adventures, but will identify with a hero who reflects the constraints of a limited sexual identity. He is likely to seek friendships exclusively with children of one sex.

When children find themselves in a world which has become polarized into male and female, they realize the limits it imposes on their potential to merge with other people. Unity requires the acceptance of sameness in the face of apparent differences, the binding of oneself with common others and a common process. Behind each developing individuality is a child's knowledge of commonality. Each of us has sought to reinforce our fragile identity by identifying with others who were like ourselves even when this tactic limited our personhood and relationships. We were afraid of intimacy with those who had conspicuous differences and sought out those who made us feel more secure in the qualities we believed we should possess. Many of us were willing to relinquish more intense encounters which challenged our sense of who we were supposed to be.

Sex roles can be very attractive in day-to-day life. They

provide each child with an instant identity within an exclusive reference group—the world of boys and men versus the world of girls and women. Such roles simplify the task of learning a unique sense of individual identity and deciding how to behave. However, on more transcendent levels, sex roles are confining and limiting. The sexual organs and the mysterious body functions that go with them become insurmountable barriers to sameness and union. Merger and loss of identity take on meanings related to sexuality. Children become afraid of losing their tenuous hold on maleness or femaleness; they become anxious about sex change and castration. Fusion with a member of the opposite sex is linked to a fear of becoming that sex. Fusion with the same sex group requires giving up that part of oneself which is allied with and attracted to the opposite sex. Even the family group is polarized by sexual anatomy and roles so that merger into its total unit becomes a far more complicated process than previously when sex differences were less relevant.

The price paid for a clarity in behavior afforded by sexual differences is the loss of a deeper consciousness of connectedness with others. *To crystallize ourselves as either male or female is to deny an earlier reality in which we are all toti-potential*, when identity was a fluid matrix unlimited by anatomical and role distinctions. Children do not give up this potential easily. Their reactions to "becoming" a little boy or girl go beyond the social simplification that process affords. At first children actively disbelieve that they will always be the same sex or that they will forever be denied the special sex functions of the other. They deal with this limitation by assuming that the situation will change in the future, that they will grow up to become the other sex or be able to change back and forth as they wish. Little boys may become fascinated with breasts and expect to grow their own. Both sexes are likely to develop fantasies about having a baby. The fantasies and dreams of pregnant fathers and mothers continue to reflect the wishes of both sexes to be pregnant and bear children. Many men develop the signs and symptoms of pregnancy such as early morning vomiting, nausea, and weight gain. Some even develop false pregnancies.[5] As boys they held on to some of their female identity. Similarly, little girls do not easily accept the absence of the magical penis. Some psychoanalysts base the entire psychology of women on the castration complex, which assumes that the girl believes she had a penis and lost it through some imagined fault of her own—usually a secret fantasy about her father. Neither child likes to lose an earlier potential totality. A common childhood fantasy is of the multisexed god—a man-woman with breasts and a penis. It is a clear expression of the wish to return to the unity that was lost.

An additional barrier now stands between the self and others, between defined social role and the dissolution of individual boundaries, between affectionate liaisons and the full merger of the love experience. The barrier is not insurmountable. The intense pleasure of family relationships can move beyond social roles and sexual taboos. But more and more the child escapes the threat of increasingly firm individual boundaries through solitary fantasy, through techniques and objects that can be controlled in solitude.

Ecstatic relationships continue, but for the post-Oedipal child they lie more and more within a personal world of fantasy. Some of the intense magic is withdrawn from the love experience. Maternal and paternal archetypes still exist in the child's inner world, but these myths become harder and harder to fuse with feelings toward the real life mother and father. The most important relationships of the child become desexualized, that is, disassociated from the intense pleasures of the body.

The child of seven or eight learns to keep these intense experiences outside the family. Social bonds increasingly emphasize support and nurturing. The developmental process of the child reinforces interaction at the expense of fusion. Joseph Chilton Pearce has described his small son's struggles to explore the vivid levels of fantasy experience without losing touch with the ordinary world of relationships. The boy was given a "G.I.

Joe" doll for his birthday. He became increasingly involved with the soldier doll and played with nothing else. But a crisis occurred when the tension between the two worlds became too frightening.

One summer day, he became even more fey than usual, withdrawn, faraway and quiet. He ate little, looking at us with the strange pitying look of one possessed of universal secrets. He would not leave the house but sat quietly with his soldier-doll, no longer playing or speaking. The spell lasted four days, when he was suddenly himself again.

Later he voluntarily, if haltingly, explained to me why he had been "so rude" those four days. It had occurred to him, in a burst of insight, that his G.I. Joe could become alive for him, as he had passionately wished and day-dreamed about so long, and that they could play together for ever and ever. But, and here he groped his way carefully, G.I. Joe would have been alive only for him, not for anyone else, and then he, my son, could no longer have been part of us, his family, or take part in the things we did.

Chilton's boy pulled himself back from a total break toward the "other world" in order not to lose the security and comfort of his family interactions. No doubt that potential still exists and will be explored again in the future. But a pattern has been laid down in which two kinds of experiencing have been firmly separated. The father's relief at his boy's "return" is evident between the lines:

The issues were clear-cut, equally real, and equally rewarding. His decision had been no light thing, weighed those silent days. Why *we* happened to win I will never know. Perhaps we rather lost. Life should be a venture of liberty with a safe harbor for return. Perhaps my son would only have entered on an adventurous path, as Don Juan the sorcerer might say, and probably that path might have been traversed more freely than we can imagine.[6]

Psychoanalysts have termed the developmental phase between six and twelve as latency. The label emphasizes quiescence, a sense of being poised on a brink, a time of waiting. It is seen as the natural and necessary outcome of intense sexual conflicts within the family, a developmental truce, and a regrouping of inner resources prior to the re-emergent sexuality of adolescence. It is as if a covert agreement has been reached within the family that certain pleasures do not belong within the child-parent relationship. The conflicts and turmoil of Oedipal relationships are further shifted to external accomplishments. The child can be praised for a good report card, a well-built model car, an interest in cooking or sewing. Relationships can revolve more and more around products, accomplishments, and acquired skills than on emotionally charged pleasures.

The behavior of children in the latency period is like that of couples who choose to be together on the basis of common interests and background. Couples who marry on the basis of such strengths enjoy solid liaisons that may last longer than marriages based on "love," but there is an entire level of relating that is left out. The dyadic ecstasies are buried in favor of harmony and adjustment. So too are post-Oedipal relationships simpler, cleaner, and more comfortable. Feelings are muted and displaced. The parent can begin to enjoy the child without being threatened by sexual probing. Parents can live vicariously through each childhood achievement and find cause outside the family for each problem in the child's behavior. The children gain too. With each new skill they have more self-assurance and control. They receive genuine recognition for their accomplishments without any of the complications that accompanied success in the Oedipal era. It is a happy if superficial truce from the less substantive but more intense aspects of earlier love.

As school-age children move forward in their quest for accomplishment, they use the same-sexed parent as their primary model. Coming out of the Oedipal triangle, they realize that the safe way to enjoy the parent of the opposite sex is to identify with the parent of the same sex, that is, by achieving intimacy vicariously. The same-sexed dyads go places together and share skills. The parents are proud to have their offspring show interest. The children enjoy the attention and have the added enjoyment of pleasing the other parent who earlier had been the object of their lust. Children who do not have a same-sexed parent to help them through this stage often lapse into confusion about their sexual identity. To learn conventional sex-role behavior, children generally need to relate to intimate family members of both sexes.

Development during latency is a trend rather than a fixed blueprint. Children are incredibly sensitive to the social forces within the family. Their new individuality and their contacts outside the home give them alternatives which never existed before. If being appreciated by parents depends on external achievements, then children can devote their energies to developing skills and products. If ecstasy makes adults uncomfortable, then it can be sought in private. If intense relationships in the family are discouraged, then they can be found elsewhere.

Ecstatic experience never totally dies out in the child. The quest for ecstasy is continuous, but its direction is sensitive to social conditions. Many children learn to keep their most intense experiences outside their family relationships. They have been turned back upon themselves, their own bodies, their own inner resources for their greatest pleasures. While social bonds emphasize support and nurturing, children also develop other worlds, both a personal inner space and a social role with peers. The toddler began the move toward solitary ecstasy and relationships outside the family. The post-Oedipal child develops talent in these areas. The great love that is preserved from the earlier years is narcissistic, a love of objects incorporated inside the self, a love of body, individuality, freedom from dependence. Sexual identity solidifies to include not only important modeling relationships with the same-sexed parent, but also a distinct preference for friends who are exclusively members of the same sex. Whenever the two sexes relate, it is self-consciously. The favorite game of cops and robbers may be played under another popular name: boys chase the girls. The separateness of the sexes in their preferences in play reflect children's needs to further define their sex roles. Only when they are quite secure in their manliness or womanliness can they leave their reassuring same-sexed friends and go off with members of the opposite sex. Some never acquire an affinity for their own sex model and spend latency attached to members of the opposite sex—as tomboy or sissy. There may also be radical changes in this pattern if the current trend toward de-emphasizing sex-role differences progresses. Nevertheless, it will probably continue to be true that most girls prefer to play with girls and vice versa.

Novels such as *Lord of the Flies* and *Butterfly Revolution* portray the intense world of latency-period children free from the constraints of family or adult authority. We all must remember the profound loves and hates of our own childhood—our feeling of worthlessness when an envied clique would not let us in, our tingle of joy at hearing our name during "choosing sides." We developed skills (baseball, spelling) so that we would be chosen and we prayed that we would be popular enough to be wanted even when we knew we were not any good at the game. Being chosen might be nice to tell Mom and Dad about, but what really mattered was not letting down the team. The group becomes pre-eminent during these years in many cultures. Street urchins, neighborhood gangs, Little League, Girl Scouts, slumber parties, camp—the high points occur as the individual loses his or her sense of self with the same-sexed group. All who belong try to dress alike, speak alike, act alike. Uniforms are popular. Clubs form long enough to set up a code of conduct, a secret greeting, and a sense of exclusiveness. It is enough to make up a list of members, hide it under a floorboard, and disband. The club does not have to be for or about anything, although it may require dramatic rituals like exchanging rings or becoming blood brothers.

Some children are more successful than others in the group mode. There are always the loners who prefer isolation—the boy who spends his time hiking alone, the girl who retreats into books. And then there are the powerful dyads. Many latency-period children develop a single friend in a passionate involvement which may be brief or long-term. Teachers are familiar with pairs who do not really look alike but are together so much and share so many mannerisms that their names are often confused. Girls will share everything—clothes, dolls, books, records. They do their hair in the same way, share all their activities, and spend their free time together. They may even feel themselves as a single unit. Walking down the street, they may wonder how anyone can tell them apart. Looking at each other, they may lose all sense of distinction.

Boys go through the same process. They too share every spare moment and experience profound merger with their friend. They may wrestle together to experience the joy of their two bodies fusing into one. They may play on the same teams, tease the same girls, climb the same trees. If one has a talent not shared by the other, both may experience shock and confusion. That activity may be dropped so that they will not be forced to confront a clear distinction between their skills.

The school years are labelled "latency" on the assumption that the more intense psychological phenomena associated with sexuality in the Oedipal and adolescent periods are underground. But it seems clear that this label is appropriate only when we discuss family relationships. Latency-period children experience intense, mystical, ecstatic events, but they are likely to keep them to themselves. They are too old to call Mommy to the bedroom for reassurance about the ghosts and witches they feel are under the bed. They have to find their own way of controlling the magic forces they experience around themselves. Similarly, they are too embarrassed to be hugged and rocked to experience warm bliss. They must find their own realms of joy. They are directed toward objective skills in the outside world. These are the years during which they acquire the work ethos, during which they gain the fundamentals of an education that will help them adapt to the requirements of their culture.

With independence comes a sense of joy at being in and with the world. Increased social pressure for activity and competence opens up many additional avenues for pleasure in the inanimate world which would never have been found from experimenting with fantasy or even relationships. Children of this age whirl in exultant play. There is the dazzle of colored lights, a new appreciation of the composition of water, the infinite crystalline structure of a leaf—there is the discovery of the general beauty and knowledge that all these things can be merged into one's identity. Work itself may carry with it the stimulation of curiosity and a joy of discovery. The search for truth, whether in the self or the world, has its own ecstatic potential. The child who plunges headlong into learning, who tries to understand reality and absorb his society's world-view, may experience the intensely pleasurable sense of merger with a body of knowledge or a skill.

Poets talk of love being inspired by a rock, a tree, a book, a flower, a star. What they mean is that the sense of wonder, awe, and bliss that begins in the arms of another is present in all of life, not just in the world of personal relationships. The seemingly infinite variety of ecstatic experience supports these insights. Wherever the child looks, no matter how pragmatic his interests, he will find that there is more beyond the real images than he could have dreamed. He cannot escape his own ecstatic potential. He must learn where it can be found, but even more important, where it is safe to be experienced. The external ideal is work. Pleasure may be taken in private. It is often felt to be forbidden. It may even have to be hidden from conscious being.

Latency-period children may learn to experiment with and control their states of consciousness as they develop their skills in all areas of life. They are likely to experience pre-relational merger states in situations unrelated to feelings of security. It is during these years that the disassociation between ecstasy and dependence in a relationship becomes patterned. Increasing individuality does not necessarily dim the potential for ecstasy; rather it changes the forms through which it is sought. Almost all talented mystics trace the beginning of their powers to these years when they learned to develop ecstatic modes that focussed outside the world of relationships.

For example, Eileen Garrett, a renowned medium, traces her

first memory of psychic ability back to childhood. She describes experiences of reading the minds of family members, predicting the future, seeing strange auras around objects and even visions. Much of the time these experiences were linked to strong emotional events in which her "talents" got her into trouble with adults, as when she accurately foretold that an unborn child would die. She describes her experience thus:

> We all have it—only of course we grow up and go to our parents first who usually say, "don't bother me; don't talk like that, you're telling stories." So you become a little fearful, afraid and possibly ashamed, and you don't do anything about it.[7]

Eileen Garrett believes that a tolerant uncle was the key to the development of her special talents. Instead of anger or disbelief at her predictions, he reacted sympathetically, saying, "Well, my child, maybe so. Who knows?" He died when she was fifteen:

> A few weeks after his death, I was sitting in my room in the evening, feeling a bit restless and unhappy, when I saw him clearly standing before me. I was surprised at his appearance of health, since before his death he had seemed feeble and worn. But he appeared young, erect, and strong. I was overjoyed at seeing him and he showed he was happy to see me . . .

Mrs. Garrett describes the tenuous nature of the magical aspects of a child's world in the face of criticism from the family. Her uncle sheltered her from other criticisms and allowed her to follow her mind into realms that she would not have dared discover otherwise. When he died, she was able to use her visionary powers to assure herself that he was all right and to confirm her own ability to reach her special mental states without anyone else giving approval.

Not only declared mystics have such experiences in childhood. Robert is a man who had profound and intense "raptures" that were at their height when he was between six and twelve. He describes suddenly being in a different place, a different world from his everyday home life. This shift was accompanied by an extraordinarily poignant and pleasurable emotion rare in such states. The feeling was of inner richness and happiness. His sense of who and where he was would disappear as this other consciousness pervaded him.

At first, these experiences came over him spontaneously. He then learned how to induce and control them. He would think about what it was like to be held as a tiny infant. His sister was six years younger than he, so that he was able to identify with her experience and delve into his own memory of what it was like. The content of his "raptures," the physical landscape, was identical to the landscape that had surrounded the home of his infancy.

He never discussed his raptures with anyone. They gradually became less and less frequent and he lost his ability to induce them. Then, in late adolescence, he had a spontaneous experience that occurred during a conversation with a friend. Suddenly he was in a world more real and marvellous than the other. There was no reason for him to return. But after that experience, he was frightened by the raptures. He felt he had to choose worlds. The other reality was too enticing and if he entered it he might never come back. Increasingly he became reticent about any heightened or exhilarating state, particularly those induced by drugs, for he felt that even his memory of rapture might take him away from reality forever. He committed himself to the more secular tasks of marrying and raising a family.

This is only a fragment of a case history. It did not occur in a clinical setting and involves a man who knew little of psychology. He experienced the loss of his "I" and felt he was gaining an entire universe through total merger of sensual and emotional experience. It was related in his own mind to the "prerelational" state in his life. His descriptions have a purity unmarred by the superstructure of a metaphysical system. He seemed to be recapitulating infantile consciousness outside of all real relationships. He never told his parents of this aspect of his reality; nor did he share his raptures with his wife, for he felt them to be a threat to family life. He had a son who had been considered a prodigy before he began school but now seemed average at age eight. Perhaps the son, too, had learned to isolate his "special" world, relating normally with peers and family and keeping his more intense experiences to himself.

Ingo Swann, an artist who has frequently experienced "astral travelling" or out-of-body moments, describes his childhood travels:

> When I was a child I used to play around by zooming out of the body and going into the earth. I was born in the Rocky Mountains and I used to like to follow the different metal veins through the mountains. I would just kind of zoom along them until they came to the surface.[8]

He too experienced the suppression of these and other abilities during his childhood and describes his present "rehabilitation" as the result of increased self-awareness and contact with spiritual teachers. He makes the link between childhood mystical experience and the ecstasy of relationships quite clear:

> As a child I could remember past lifetimes, and I was always interested in the aesthetics of the universe: flowers, animals, the mountains and streams, the cycles of the seasons. I would meditate on these relationships and feel how beautiful they were. Later on, I became more interested in the same thing that goes on between people—spiritual interactions that take place.

Swann is unusual in eventually including relationships as a focus for his ecstatic experience.

Retrospective accounts from men and women who have a stake in remembering (or inventing) the occult aspects of their childhood are less helpful evidence than descriptions from children themselves. Most adults do have vague recollections of a childhood filled with a variety of ecstatic states that have become non-relevant and even absurd from the point of view of a more bounded reality. Unfortunately, the private ecstatic experiences of latency-age children are hesitantly discussed even by parents who have glimpses of their raptures. It violates their comfortable focus on the external world and forces an awareness on both child and parent that they are growing further apart from each other in some ways that really matter. The child agrees not to tell; everyone else not to listen. But underneath the quiet and the truce, the ecstatic part of their relationship simmers. And if the child chooses to reveal his inner magic world to the parent, the relational wellspring of that world is laid bare and each must face the other fully and openly.

A father related the following experience of this kind to the authors:

> My daughter is almost eight years old. We have always been close and loving, but for a long time our talk had been of progress in school, her friends, her feelings about her teachers. We did things together. I thought there was little to improve our relationship.
>
> One evening I was seized by a vague feeling that there was something I didn't understand about her. We happened to be the only two members of the family at home, so we listened to music and sipped tea together. We talked of routine things for a while. Then I asked her what was happening inside of her. She began to tell me about her "flying" experiences. She said she could decide when to leave her body and fly. She wore a special costume, an outfit that sounded like a feminine superman with wings. She had adventures which were like stories in books or on TV. She said they weren't dreams because they could happen during the day or as she lay awake in bed. She sometimes did it when she was bored, but they were not fundamentally escapist flights. It was exciting, she said. Rapturous. A feeling of losing herself and gaining great power. She sat on my lap and showed me how she did it; she started breathing deeply and rhythmically until she was in a motionless trance that lasted five minutes or more. Having her on my lap in this state was an extraordinarily intimate experience.

The girl of eight has discovered her own private ecstasy which she had not shared with her parents and probably would never have mentioned if her father had sought not to go beyond what he thought was a close and warm relationship. The flying may be a disguised desire to sleep with her father and replace her mother in his bed. Surely that may have been in the father's attitude, too, as he sought a mature relationship with his female companion that evening. But flying was more than that for her. It was her private, self-discovered path to ecstasy. It placed self-transcendence in her control, that is, outside of a relationship. When she communicated the experience to her father, she re-opened the potential to have a loss-of-"I" experience with him in their love relationship.

Most families would have trouble handling such a renewed flowering of the father/daughter relationship on an intimate, ecstatic dimension beyond common interests and admiration of skills. Sexuality and the possibility of incest loom up to inhibit cross-sex relationships within the family as adolescence approaches. Sexual feelings cannot be artificially separated from love relationships any more easily than physical pleasure can be eliminated from ecstasy. Profound intimacy may be frightening indeed to parents and children who are not sure of their ability to control their sexual feelings.

Unfortunately, there are almost no histories of the ongoing development of normal childhood ecstatic states. Psychological examination of children may occasionally uncover such material, but it is likely to be labelled "daydream" or "pathology" depending on how vividly it is presented and how much it dominates "normal" functioning. For example, it is taken for granted that children have imaginary playmates and fantasy dwelling places. Every parent has seen his child go into a trance state (although he might be shocked to have it clinically described as that). We seldom confront the fantasy and explore its potential as an ecstatic voyage for the child. We are more likely to react with concern and embarrassment. The child psychologist routinely tells parents not to worry about the conversations they overhear between their child and his fantasy playmate. "He'll grow out of it if we don't make it into an issue." A teacher may attempt to harness "creativity" in writing or dramatics, but even then the message is likely to be, "Don't share your other reality with us unless you carefully say you are pretending."

Patrick and Richard Noone have shown how the educational system of the Temiar people in the jungle interior of Malaya emphasizes rather than discourages the children's fantasies. All the members of this tribe openly share their dreams in daily councils. To the Temiar, dreams are as real and important as waking experiences. Almost all group actions rest on the predictive power of dream contents.

> If a man dreams of a particular spot in the river, he will fish there. If his dreams suggest a valley or settlement in which he should seek a bride, he will look there. I have met men who dream up mechanical inventions such as fish traps, complicated puzzles, decorative patterns, medicinal remedies. Their poetry, their songs, their music, their dances, are all dream inspired.[9]

What is unique about this tribe is the active group support and validation of the dream experience in all ages, but particularly in the young, who are trained in dreaming and in dream interpretation. Mornings begin with dream recitations during which the children listen to their parents and other adults describe their dreams to one another. They too are expected to describe their dreams and participate in the interpretative sessions. Children join in decision-making councils; their dreams are given equal weight with all others present.

Our own culture tends to think of dreams as phenomena whose content and form may be useful in understanding motivation, providing creative clues, or predicting the future. Psychiatry uses dreams extensively as conduits from the unconscious, but even then there is no attempt made to help patients transform their dreams as they occur. The dream state is differentiated from other forms of consciousness such as trances, out-of-body experiences, and visions. It is taken to be beyond conscious influence. If a child reports an unusual mental phenomenon to his parents, the immediate question is, "Were you dreaming?" And if the answer is affirmative, then everyone relaxes, for the content of dreams is taken to be non-pathological and relatively unimportant for pragmatic functioning.

The Temiars use dreams in a quite different way. Not only are dreams used for guidance, but members of the tribe learn actively to manipulate their own dreams. In the morning dream inquests, the dreamer is questioned about his own role within the dream; the child is taught how to dream "correctly," how to vary his actions in future dreams, how to rectify inappropriate actions.

> To dream correctly, the child is told he must never be afraid. If he dreams of smoke, he must not avoid it as he would smoke during his waking hours because it stings the eyes. He must go boldly into dream smoke, for deep inside it he may find something of value, perhaps even the spirit of the smoke which he can overcome and bend to his own will . . . The Temiar child is told that if he dreams he is soaring or falling, he must let himself go, as these sensations represent the efforts of one of his souls to get free from his body; but if he is afraid of hitting the bottom or of reaching too high, the soul will be impeded in its need to arrive somewhere.

The child is taught to encounter the images which frighten him, even if they are his own parents. He is told to exploit sexual opportunities even if they involve incest. Activities which are taboo in waking life are allowed in dreams.

The tribal shaman is chosen for his skill in dream life and other trance states. He acts as intermediary between the spirit world and the group. All Temiars are adept at trance states and familiar with the spirit world. The shaman is simply the most expert. He leads the group in their rigorous explorations of the world of dreams. The entire group cooperates in supporting the ecstatic quest in order to comprehend and control experiences in dreams, no matter how exhilarating or terrifying.

Most of us are reticent to support and understand these aspects of a child's experience. We recognize the hidden, magic world of the child's mind and try to deal with it by insisting that the child learn to focus on reality and forget the dream experience. We discourage occult and mystical potential when it does appear. We are afraid of its dangers. For example, in Thomas Tryon's novel *The Other* a woman teaches her grandson the ecstatic "game" of flying in the body of a crow. The two form an extraordinarily intense relationship, but the boy's talents get out of control. His ability to alter his consciousness leads him to perform bizarre and dangerous acts leading to numerous deaths. It is quite clear that the "magic" abilities are taken to be the gifts of the devil; only evil results from the boy's giving up his soul to another. Every culture is aware of the potential dangers in its ecstatic traditions. They provide a guru or shaman to guard against the enemy, the embodiment of evil. In *The Other*, the grandmother warned the boy, but she simply did not know how far he had gone; she could not protect him from his runaway talent. We do not believe children can control ecstatic experience.

Homo sapiens is a remarkably complex and flexible organism. From the time that he begins to move outside his mother's arms, the child is developing in directions that are determined more by social than biological factors. The forms that love and ecstasy will take are inevitably influenced by the kinds of relationships available to the child and the ecstatic techniques which he is taught or accidentally acquires. As soon as an "I" emerges, he will be striving to maintain relationships with other people, for he needs them to survive. Every child finds his own way to capture and hold the magic feelings that vibrate from pre-relational states in order to re-awaken the sense of merger in group, dyad, or totality. Some children work on intense relationships inside the family. Others turn to peer relationships. Yet most children, like Robert who exchanged his raptures for the calmer world of reality, use the latency years to hide their ecstasies. The longing for total merger is tucked away within, faintly felt, an unfulfilled longing for an ideal forever lost. The sense of the Other is part of oneself and the universe has drifted further and further away. Bittersweet longing for a vaguely remembered magical world with an Other is hidden beneath a film of social skills and expectations until puberty when a fresh drive for union emerges and is shaped through the tumultuous relationships of adolescence.

6

Ecstatic Relationships in Adolescence

MOST of us like to think of our lives as being continuous. By assuming that we are the same person now that we were ten years ago and will be ten years from now, we gain a sense of control over our development and maintain an illusion of being able to understand our existence. There are moments in our lives, however, when we are forced to recognize a single event as a discrete and separate entity which does not necessarily fit in with all the other moments of our lives in a harmonious pattern. At these times the continuous stream of activity is disrupted. Things are no longer taken for granted. We cannot assume that the next event or the next stage will follow inevitably. Each moment suddenly acquires an unknown potential, for it could carry us in new and unexpected directions through which we might evolve a new sense of self complete with new and unexplored roles.

Although adolescence is a developmental phase that may last ten years or more, it is also a "moment" in our lives. It is a period of profound disruption when our bodies do not simply grow, but rather become transformed; when our roles do not just shift, but lock into new places with life-long consequences.

Gurdjieff experimented with exercises which would stimulate

the individual to increase self-awareness and self-understanding. He developed "stop" exercises, like the childhood game of "freeze" in which everybody runs about until one calls "freeze" and the others have to stop in whatever positions they find themselves. Gurdjieff trained adults to play this game within their minds by having them concentrate on the exact state of the body while performing a physical act or by trying to observe the state of consciousness moment by moment as it occurred. In an even more difficult exercise, Gurdjieff asked his followers to attempt to reconstruct each of the activities of the day immediately before going to bed without losing themselves in free associations.[1]

Gurdjieff's exercises are akin to other "awakening" techniques which attempt to bring the individual to a new awareness of himself and his universe. Meditation and worship often require concentration on one point or one single object leading to a fresh vision. Characteristically, the individual first experiences a heightened sense of "I" but ultimately reaches a state in which the "I" and all usual perceptions of reality dissolve.

It requires extraordinary discipline to perceive distinct elements in the ongoing flow of ordinary consciousness. Such games challenge the fabric of social givens and subvert what behavioral scientists call the "average expectable environment" upon which our ordinary social acts depend. They create artificial transition points which challenge our existing assumptions. Good teachers use similar techniques when they act or answer in unexpected ways; the sudden "shock" of their action can propel the student into new perceptions.

The problem with gimmicks that provide a fresh consciousness is simply that they may not go beyond being games. In times of boredom and loss of meaning they may become faddish. To use them honestly would require changing a life style. Their practitioners are often unwilling to do so unless they are supported by a powerful leader or a strong tradition. Thus gimmicks soon lose their impact. Nevertheless, we all have mind-shaking events organically built into our lives which we cannot ignore.

The inevitable rhythms of our biological life cycle can create powerful transitions which may shake our illusion of continuity and lead us to an altered life style or heightened consciousness. Most conspicuously, birth and death shatter our straightforward interpretation of daily affairs. At such moments our personal and social equilibrium shifts. Change gets out of control. The pattern of our lives is suddenly exposed as related to profound life forces and unanticipated levels of consciousness rather than to our domestic and work routines.

The rituals and ceremonies surrounding the great rites of passage are the sacred moments in which men contemplate cosmic rhythms, re-evaluate their awareness of their place in the universe, and explore hidden meanings of the life cycle. These are times when at least briefly there is the potential of being reborn. During these rituals ecstatic consciousness becomes the dominant reality whether in the form of group merger or transmitted through the role of someone like a shaman. In contrast to these sacred peaks the everyday duties of society are profane moments.[2] They outweigh the sacred in sheer bulk, but not necessarily in importance to individual members of the community. In our own culture the meaning of birth and death and the other rites of passage are often obscured by medical and religious technologies which have not been sacralized. Even so these periods of discontinuity in our ordinary flow of existence are moments when the sharing of ecstatic experience meets the least resistance from the community. Extraordinary behavior is accepted and even encouraged during such transitions. A confrontation with birth or death is like a biological game of freeze in which an individual's relationship to former experience is suddenly altered. Unlike consciousness games which can be discarded when they prove too difficult, the birth or death of a loved one actually does alter reality for a time, perhaps for a very long time, until the individual adjusts to his new world as his profane state. At the height of these periods the individual is primed for ecstatic consciousness without needing the preparation that ecstatic traditions seek to provide.

Puberty is one of the classic rites of passage. The individual is reborn both in his own transformed body and experience and in the eyes of his community. The ritual acceptance of the new adult into society is often structured in terms of death and rebirth and may include a journey through a womb space or a symbolic death and resurrection. The biological process is time specific; the social process may take place in a ritual lasting several days or over a period of years as in our own culture. In whatever form it always marks a major transition when we are most able to reach beyond the world of the profane and grasp our sacred environment and selves.

Puberty has been defined as the "condition of having become functionally capable of procreating offspring." [3] It is important that the culture train youths in adult responsibilities before they become parents. When parenthood and full adult responsibilities follow immediately upon sexual maturity, the transition from childhood to full adult status is rapid indeed, for puberty occurs with remarkable swiftness. The genitals and sexual characteristics enlarge rapidly at the same time that the rest of the body undergoes sudden growth which determines the final size and approximate shape of the individual.

Adolescence, in contrast to puberty, is defined as "the process of growing up; the period which extends from childhood to manhood or womanhood; ordinarily considered as extending from 14-25 in males and 12-21 in females." [4] The psychological and social changes of adolescence are longer in term and relatively more gradual for most people in our culture. Adolescence is a bridge which both child and society use to re-adjust and integrate the "reborn" individual into the conservative stream of the society. The "rebirth" may be experienced most profoundly at a point removed from puberty if physical and social maturity are separated, as generally they are in our culture.

Adolescents' awareness of their rapidly changing bodies forces a similar awareness of a continually changing self-image. There is an almost compulsive need for daily self-observation in order to stay in touch with both who they are and how they are viewed by the world around them. People react to their new size and particularly to their new sexuality in totally unexpected ways. A boy who was dominant over his friends as an eleven year old may suddenly find himself to be subordinate to most of his peers who matured physically before he did. An unpopular girl may suddenly find herself the center of attention because she flowers nicely at just the right time; her popularity may die off just as rapidly if she turns unfashionably plump. The variable growth and maturation rates of puberty radically shift former friendship alliances, particularly because peer conversations at puberty tend to have so much to do with sex whether explicitly or implicitly. When all the other girls exchange stories about their adventures purchasing their first brassiere, their one flat-chested friend may turn toward other and perhaps younger girls who like her have not yet graduated out of their undershirts. The boy who has suddenly grown three inches in a summer may gain rapid success as a basketball star; the agile athlete who does not have any pubic hair to show off in the locker room may lose the former admiration of his peers. It takes a remarkably talented leader to maintain his dominant position over friends who mature before he does. And it takes a strong friendship to hold two friends through puberty if they do not mature at similar rates.

The problems of puberty are not restricted to new ways in which older people react to youth. Teenagers find their inner experience shifting as they try to accept and deal with their new bodies and its sensations. A girl may be startled to have men (or older boys) whistle at her. Up until now she has thought of herself as just a little girl. Teenagers discover that they are being valued for traits they were never expected to have before. Often these seem to be merely external and are not easily integrated into one's consciousness. A young girl wonders whether a boy really loves her or is just interested in her breasts. Pubescent teenagers often feel detached from their bodies and even from their accomplishments as though feeling they do not really belong inside this strange phenomenon.

Along with physical and social, there are also internal changes as hormones readjust and sexual drives emerge with unsuspected power. Teenagers have to take possession of all their new functions. They must integrate their new moods with their unfamiliar body and altered relationships. They must learn to handle themselves and their drives in socially acceptable patterns they never needed before.

Erik Erikson has pointed out that the developmental task of adolescence is the crystallization of identity in both the psychological and social sense. Adolescents must somehow pull together the multiple strands of "I-ness" gathered throughout childhood. They must weave these fibers into the new context of physical maturity and find an answer to the mystery of who they are. The process is similar to the congealing of a sense of "I" out of the dyadic and group consciousness in the third year of life. Then the transition to individuality was from out of the merged consciousness of the infant. In adolescence, identity is more specific; it is the discovery of one's particular nature, personality, ideals, and values in relation to all other self-fragments and all other people with whom the adolescent must relate. There have been other surges toward fresh re-definition—thus the transitions of losing the first tooth or learning how to read, for example—but they were short-term and partial. The child rapidly adapted to these new images of himself and the world. Puberty and especially its social ramifications create a whole new field for identity transformation. Biology provides its own push toward a continuing psychological definition with a force that makes most mystical Ways seem tame in comparison.

The struggle for identity in adolescence is not a simple or a silent task. Its difficulty is reflected in its length. In our society it takes approximately the same amount of time as the rest of childhood. There is a great deal of inner and outer turmoil that seems to be an inevitable by-product of the adolescent quest for identity. Perhaps only in pregnancy is there a comparable psychic outpouring with such emotional liability and such uncontrollable fantasy life.

Disturbed behavior is so intense during adolescence that it is virtually impossible for clinicians to distinguish between psychopathology and intense normality. The term "adolescent turmoil" is used to label the personal and social confusion that frequently occurs. The related term "identity diffusion" describes the adolescent's inability to bring the elements of "I" and "self" together in some kind of harmonious relationship to one another. Sometimes teenagers feel so fragmented that they cannot competently act or think. Some adopt a "negative identity" organized in opposition to the values which have characterized earlier childhood; and in this way they hope to resolve the tension they experience so acutely. Adolescents are already overloaded with mind-shattering input from their changing bodies and new social roles and yet they seek even more disassociating experience. They join extremist groups, adopt bizarre ideologies, and experiment with powerful drugs. These involvements may help temporarily to alleviate the turmoil and diffusion within.

Adolescents must confront the meaning of being an adult in their home culture. If they are afraid of displacing older siblings, worry about competition with same-sexed parents, or despise the adults by whom they have been raised, they must seek alternative pathways of success. Similarly, if they feel unworthy or cannot gain acceptance as their new self, or if the friction between the old and new roles becomes too great, they may seek a world in which their identity starts anew in their present state as a partially formed adult.

A group may support this negative identity and help define the adolescent's struggle against authority. Adolescents growing up in a society where their elders prize visible success are particularly apt to feel paralyzed by their inability to compete with adults. But if they set up new structures and rules, they can feel competent in other ways. For example, the older generation cannot evaluate the unknown realm of psychedelics. Thus in the sixties the younger generation found an area in which they were more knowledgeable and experienced than their elders. All their heroes were "under thirty" and relatively easy to emulate.

The adolescent's search for identity involves far more than

"adolescent turmoil," "identity diffusion," and "negative identity." It also means exploring ecstatic potential, for ecstatic experience is an important part of self-discovery. Teenagers experiment with solitary, dyadic, and group modes to see which fit best with their emerging adult identity. Typically, there is a frenzied investigation of many kinds of consciousness-changing experiences. Adolescents with no sense of direction may slam their fingers in doors or burn their arms with cigarettes to bring about an intense encounter with a world that too often seems unreal because of the profound changes that have occurred in their lives, bodies, and feelings. Drugs, group movements, arcane spiritual paths, or academic devotions are passionately explored and equally passionately discarded. Of all the stages of human development, adolescence seems most willing to risk all in the quest for ecstasy, to renounce materialism, and to take daring risks, physically, chemically, and spiritually.

The ecstatic experiences of adolescents often seem silly, even sacrilegious, to adults. They are often poorly utilized, immature, and may be dangerously indulged. Adults who support the mystical knowledge provided by psychedelic drugs are dismayed by youths of sixteen who follow their first "trip" with fifty more. A yoga master too must struggle with young followers who experience genuine but fragmented and sporadic bliss through such discipline. Thus Omar Garrison tells of a guru who was training a select group of young disciples for a year or more to prepare them for ritual ecstasy with women in the Tantra Yoga tradition:

> All went well, I can tell you, until maithuna. As you may know, the necessary thing in this practice is *jitendriya*—control of the senses, especially control of the seed or semen. Emission is not allowed for any reason.
>
> But one of the boys—a Pashu infected with the taint of the Kali Age, did not restrain his bindu as I have taught him. Instead, he is spending his seed, like one devoid of all dharma. Shiva! Shiva! Even a worse thing. To the others of the circle he is saying, "This is very jolly. Let us indulge."

Is there need for saying more? They all were discharging with shouts like players at a polo match or a gymkhana. So the fruit of their long *sadhana* was lost. It is still lost. They must find some other path to liberation.[5]

The vast majority of adults, who are not meaningfully involved as teachers or practitioners of ecstatic traditions, can afford to be more complacent about the excesses of youth. Most treat adolescent ecstasies with a mixture of annoyance and condescension. They take refuge in the probability that the "child" will grow out of it. They reason that they themselves once felt possessed by uncontrollable feelings which seemed startlingly genuine at the time but were based on nothing more than fantasy or physical sensation. Now they have extracted themselves from these visions and become productive individuals. Yet even those adults whose youthful ecstasies have not entirely been dismissed can rarely help feeling unquiet at an adolescent's own experiences. In hindsight they feel the ecstatic moments that come so rarely in adulthood were "wasted on youth."

Of all the intense and confusing new sensations that bombard the teenager after puberty, sex is perhaps the most difficult to integrate with past experience and future expectations. Genital sensations suddenly preoccupy thoughts and fantasies more than at any earlier period. The sexuality of a child of five was diffuse and had a loving relationship at its core. In later childhood sex play carried with it as much ambivalent curiosity as pleasure. But the sudden sexual drive which accompanies the ability to procreate is disassociated from any personal rhythm, patterned relationship, or system of sublimation or release. Throughout adolescence the individual will experiment with ways to use sex for ecstatic solitary and perhaps group experiences and eventually in one-to-one relationships.

At first sex is primarily masturbation. Even for those who have been playing with their genitals since they were six or earlier, masturbation takes on a new interest. Orgasm and particularly emission are the main focus of their attention. Changes in size and shape and texture of the genitals add to the fascination. Hair, fluids, and the more dramatic expansion of penis or labia with excitation can confuse or thrill the exploring adolescent. For some pubescent children the pleasure and guilt of masturbation come to dominate their entire waking life and even intrude upon their sleep. When done in secrecy and isolation, masturbation is a magnified experience of the ecstatic world of latency. It is better and simpler than "flying." It supplants other forms of magic. It is instant pleasure over which there is individual control. Like ecstasies of the latency period, its experience does not depend on an Other. Fantasy supplies relationships as they are needed. Real people would only be a confusing intrusion on the new-found world of secret parts and personal places.

But inevitably this powerful new drive challenges the tendency in childhood to disassociate ecstatic experience from relationships. Sex almost always has a human object, even if just in masturbatory fantasy. Sex pushes toward the reunion of ecstasy and relationship in the love experience. Few find masturbation the ultimate sexual pleasure. Most adolescents sooner or later want to test the thrill with other people, to explore the body of another, give pleasure as well as gain it. Masturbation may be reliable, ecstatic, and fascinating, but after it has been explored and comprehended it may begin to seem two-dimensional. The adolescent yearns to go beyond self-directed pleasures and share his body with another, but he finds himself laden with old, non-ecstatic dependency, with relational scripts that no longer seem appropriate but still persist in directing his behavior. Most of all he discovers how very difficult it is to go beyond a thinly disguised self-love into a true encounter with an Other.

The first shared sexual experiences of a young adolescent are likely to be with a member or members of the same sex. These are less threatening, for the Other is closer to the self in that he has a more familiar body. It is misleading to label such activities homosexuality, for they have little or no prophetic value about the sexual orientation the adolescent will choose for the rest of his life. These encounters are explorations. The adolescent wants to discover the body of others and test his against theirs. There may be a great deal of bravado and little intimacy in such an encounter. Pubescent boys have contests to see who can "come" first or whose semen will squirt the farthest. Excitement and competition may well be the dominant emotions. Any ecstasy experienced during orgasm is likely to be isolated, even hidden, though in a particularly well-formed group there may be an experience of union and camaraderie with the others, that is, a group merger. Similarly, special friends may participate in strange, magical encounters in which two boys or two girls have an intimate, loving sexual exchange. They may pretend they are of opposite sexes and play at being married. One may be considerably older than the other and initiate his younger friend. Often the two are like identical twins, exploring an objectified vision of self in the other, discovering the wonders of their own bodies in a form that they can see from new angles and stimulate in fresh ways.

The drive to understand the mysteries of sex and to enjoy the excitement of arousal are far more powerful than the prohibitions placed by society on sexual activity. If adolescents cannot be direct and open in their explorations, they will be secretive. They are now equipped with enough intellectual function to rationalize their thinking and doing. They can confess to sinful things as a chance to talk about them, pray for forgiveness as a chance to ruminate, focus on chastity as an opportunity to concentrate energy on sexual function (if not release). They can also deny, even to themselves, the fact that certain activities are sexual in intent. They can blatantly rebel and justify their activities as being important because they are forbidden, thus protecting themselves from an admission that they are confused and want to explore and learn. They can blindly and passionately fall in love because they feel love is sanctioned while cooler passion is forbidden.

A great deal of sexual activity among adolescents will not culminate in orgasm or coitus. Cultural standards vary considerably. American teenagers in the past few decades have indulged in a great deal of heavy petting, an activity encouraged by the automobile, which provides an excellent place for boy and girl to be together though it is not conveniently designed for intercourse. Similarly, the homosexual play of pubescent girls in particular may consist more in caressing than anything else. Encounters tend to be so fleeting and relationships so unstable that the gratification is not as profound or lasting as in more mature sexuality. Focus and obsession tend to converge on the arousal states. The dirty jokes, the confessionals, the lies, all center on what was done, not on the quality of gratification or interpersonal sharing that was experienced.

Petting and necking may be enjoyed for their own sake even while the experience of mutual orgasm is months, perhaps years, in the future. Adolescence is a time to discover external skills and develop unfamiliar behavior patterns. The relationship that fails, or the date that is a painful embarrassment to both parties, may be the most valuable in teaching the participants how to proceed in future relationships. Long-term love is hardly a realistic issue for most mid-adolescents. Their identity is in such a state of flux that they need a variety of companions with whom to test various aspects of their potential personality. They do not want to merge completely with any one other, for they would then find themselves in a limited field with delineated potentials. They prefer to leave open the mystery of identity and experiment with many short-term but intense relationships. To merge is to risk becoming submerged, to return to a dependency state like childhood.

Our childhood struggles for sexual identity in the competitive Oedipal matrix has taught us that sexual flirtation can be risky and even frightening. In adolescence we are still inhibited from plunging fully into a single, long-term, heterosexual love encounter and yet we sense and soon know that the mutuality of heterosexual intercourse can be far more pleasurable than the sensations we achieve on our own. The experience of sexual pleasure in a relationship constantly hovers before adolescents as a possibility toward which they should work—and yet there are so many obstacles, both in sexual techniques and in the subtleties of relationships. Relationships, or conversely, sex may be set aside while the other is explored. More than sex, adolescents may want love and respect—but not as these were known in childhood, not through stable and dependent relationships with people they have known all their lives.

Adolescence is a time of experimental interactions with others. Family relationships have atrophied. The adolescent sees "child" reflected in the eyes of his mother and father. He needs to grow and develop competence. To the extent that the adolescent can still experience merger with his parents, he still finds himself trapped within the boundaries of their definition of him. He will inevitably return to the patterns of his childhood in these new relationships, but he needs to leap toward the unknown Others to feel newborn, to embroider new designs on top of his old patterns. Frequently adolescents choose group merger to help them find a strong identity outside the family which offers alternatives to childhood roles. They also become involved in profound, searching friendships.

In adolescence the "I" is in constant flux and experimentation. Each new encounter, each new event, might redirect or transform identity, that is, create a path which will lead the person to a new place. Government class may evoke fantasies about law school, court, a judgeship. An hour later, gym class may be regarded as the first step to joining the football team, gaining a college scholarship, glorying in the fame and fortune of a shaving commercial. The choice between trying out for cheerleading or the school play, between dating Tom versus Dick may (in both fantasy and reality), make all the difference in shaping one potential identity rather than another. As Robert Frost reflects:

Two roads diverged in a wood, and I—
I took the one less traveled by,
*And that has made all the difference.**

Adolescents, more dramatically than children or adults, are in the process of becoming that of which they dream—but as they make their choice of dreams, friends, roads, they eliminate things they *might have been* and come closer to a sense of who they *are* and *will be.* Each adventure seems like a "journey to a place with no name," like "riding the steed of non-being to the place where nothing is." Each step may form a chain leading to that magical future in which identity will solidify or lead to nowhere. Neither alternative will be entirely welcome. There is a constant temptation to enter initiation rites and irrevocably delineate the final pathway. Many adolescents choose to do this. Others stay open to the kaleidoscope of changing roles.

Two individuals, young or old, create a new union each time they face one another in true openness to their own and the other's uniqueness at that place and moment. But the "I"-ridden notion of firm boundaries is less of a liability for the adolescent than for those at other stages in the life cycle. Children work hard to find a secure base within the family. Adults struggle to maintain a place for themselves in the larger society. Once the bewildering fluidity of identity crystallizes, an individual thinks he knows his "I," his universe, and the people to whom he relates. The breathtaking freshness of new love mellows or even disintegrates when patterns and expected roles develop. The already formed individual tends to classify people on the basis of past alliances or future perspectives rather than on wondrous hopes for the present. The adolescent, mid-way between the framework of family and that of adult identity, may encounter each new being as a potential partner in the creation of a new universe of experience.

* From "The Road Not Taken" from *The Poetry of Robert Frost*, edited by Edward Connery Lathem. Copyright 1916, © 1969 by Holt, Rinehart and Winston, Inc. Copyright 1944 by Robert Frost. Reprinted by permission of Holt, Rinehart and Winston, Inc.

Love is the overwhelming ecstasy of adolescence. In the most general sense it is love of all the world and every animal, person, and thing in it. Adolescents explore a variety of ecstatic traditions and yet relationships are what seem to hold the most potential. Sexual maturity alters the childhood emphasis on dependency as the prime emotion between people. New kinds of relationships outside the family may be initiated by physical desire but soon take on a greater experiential richness. Other ecstatic paths are sought when old patterns get in the way of new ecstatic relationships—for example, when the individual is strong enough to merge with a deity but still afraid to attempt a relationship with a person. But during adolescence there is seldom a permanent detour from the search for ecstatic relationships. The Other is the great, mysterious bridge toward ecstatic experience.

Ecstatic experience is not necessarily of positive value for the firm establishment of individual identity. There is a strong undertow toward loss of "I" in adolescence precisely because the task of self-definition is so difficult. The social impact of gender identity is the cutting edge of the process of self-definition. Puberty transforms boy into man and girl into woman. Sexual feelings and orgasm lead in the opposite direction, namely, toward union of opposites, dissolution of personal boundaries, temporary loss of awareness of the distinction between male and female. Love that is truly merger can threaten a tentative new gender identity.

Intense dyadic love relationships remind the adolescent of the frightening closeness of childhood in which the self had little awareness and virtually no power or mobility. The following history of a mature man reviewing the progression of his love experiences reflects the problems confronting the adolescent who is being moved by forces he cannot yet control or even perceive:

I was eighteen and had just broken up with a girl with whom I had felt secure but not passionately involved. I was walking toward my home when I saw a girl walking toward me. The breeze was blowing her blond hair across her face and shoulders in a way that immediately excited me. I was caught up in a feeling of knowing that this was the person with whom I could experience the love I longed for. As she came closer, I felt a wave of panic roll through me. The woman was my mother.

I had been dating girls who were dark and thin for several years. Yet all the time I had a fantasy of someone that would be perfect for me. It was not that this apparition was identical with my mother. Some of the qualities were different. But there was an essence that I needed and of which I was afraid.

When I was twenty-five I began to date voluptuous blond beauties. They were closer to my dream than the thin, dark girls of my earlier period, but they were more a parody than the thing itself. Then one night I woke up sweating and petrified. My girl friend was holding me loosely around the chest. I kept apart from her the rest of the night and stopped the relationship.

I finally married a woman who is like my mother in many ways. She possesses qualities that would have frightened me in adolescence, but which I seem to need now that I have come to terms with my childhood needs.

As an adolescent, this man could not integrate his childhood emotions with his more mature desires. It took years for him to resolve his conflicts and ambivalences around women and form an ecstatic dyadic relationship.

We emerge from childhood into adolescence with the sense of an ecstatic past which, if we dare, can be reopened. We fall in love with visions, taste the bliss of orgasm, plumb the private depths of other minds. We nibble at the past and let portions of it become part of our future as well. Occasionally we find a person in whom everything can be combined, who heals our earliest and deepest wound, whom we can love. And then we can struggle and pray for the ecstasy of discovery to last long enough so that a social fabric can be developed which will allow the potential for ecstasy to continue and for our personal love tradition to develop.

Adolescent turmoil, diffusion, and the drive toward negative identity all help to shape love choices and ecstatic preferences. Each individual develops his unique way of loving, but in the process love in adolescence tends toward three polarized ecstatic relationship patterns, archetypes which are seldom realized in their pure forms but rather as tendencies toward which many relationships move. The basic patterns are *infatuation, erotic attachment,* and *friendship.* At this stage they are virtually impossible to integrate into one relationship although they can be simultaneously experienced by one person in three separate relationships. All three have ecstatic possibilities but also striking limitations.

Infatuation is a kind of love that has been an obsessive concern of our culture for centuries. The Bible, Dante, Shakespeare, Goethe, all sensed its sublime aspects. Dante used Beatrice as his sublime mediator between earth and heaven. His inspiration came from the overwhelming emotion he experienced after seeing Beatrice as a young girl. Similarly, the love between Shakespeare's Romeo and Juliet led ultimately to civil peace after a period of friction, but this abstract theme of ennobling love is set in the context of a quite credible adolescent passion. Only moments before Romeo falls in love with Juliet (after the briefest glimpse of her at a crowded party), he has been professing his enduring love for another girl. Hector Berlioz likewise has told of an adolescent love that began after only a brief encounter:

> The moment I set eyes on her I felt an electric shock; in fact I fell in love with her, desperately, hopelessly. I had no wishes, no hopes, I had no idea what was the matter with me, but I suffered acutely and spent my nights in sleepless anguish.[6]

Havelock Ellis, one of the first and foremost psychologists in the area of sex and sexual love, has related his first love experience at the age of twelve. After the girl he was in love with had departed from the summer college where they had found each other, he says:

> I never saw Agnes again. I never made any effort to see her. I never mentioned her name; no one knew that I even thought of her. But for

four years her image moved and lived within me, revealing myself to myself. I never pictured to myself any joy of bodily contact with her or cherished any sensuous dreams. Yet I was devoured by a boy's pure passion.[7]

There are endless anecdotes of this kind from famous and unknown people which describe the psychotic reality of these extraordinary pseudo-relationships. Popular comic and TV culture uses a delightful shorthand for this experience: a multicolored explosion surrounding an exclamatory "POW!" We talk of such lovers as "starry-eyed," losing their heads, blind, struck dumb, possessed, as if they have somehow been transformed against their will (and better interests) by an external force.

Perhaps we denigrate the definition of love by including this strange, transcendent madness within its boundaries. We may speak of it as a crush, as first love, calf love, or puppy love, but condescending tags cannot hide the powerful ecstasies in these relationships which rival all other interaction experiences in their power. Such "crushes" have inspired some of our greatest poetry and brought individuals to the pinnacle of human courage as well as to the depths of despair. These love experiences may not suit a calm and rational view of human relationships, but calling them anything less than love denies the most profound feelings we may have in a ten-year period of our lives.

At the core of the experience of falling in love is the lack of any actual contact with the real love object. Instant attachment is dependent on the mystery of a glance or the sheerest touch of flesh rather than on intimate conversation and endless lovemaking. It is an experience of symbiosis restricted to fantasy, an unbounded condition where the object is entirely a shell filled with the projection of the lover. The object is made to fulfill needs that the lover dare not gratify in his own being in the real world he sees around him. The relationship is like the prerelational dyad of the one year old in which individual identity was unformed and no realistic recognition of an Other was possible because self and Other were the same. There is a poignant fear of discovering the real qualities of the beloved, a fear that with recognition the ecstasy will end. Thus a lover may follow his beloved on a bus, yet never attempt to introduce himself, preferring to live with fantasy rather than take his chances with reality. It is no accident that the great lovers in this mode rarely consummate the relationship. They do not want to lose the dream.

The Ravishment of Lol Stein is a fictional account of a young woman who spends most of her time in a vague dream world in which she remembers an event from her youth.[8] She follows a stranger and succeeds in manipulating him according to her desires, persuading him to enter her fantasy and act out her unusual expectations of a relationship. Few real-life lovers would be so cooperative, for the chances of becoming infatuated with someone who is actually what he seems in the eyes of the lover are slight. In the best tales of intense adolescent love, the lovers are either thwarted by forces beyond their control or die before learning to know each other as more than archetypal fantasies.

The stimulus for falling in love can be a setting, a dress, a particular face, a smile, the quality of figure or gait, any part of the shell that induces the merger experience. A glimpse is enough. Like the hypnotic subject who may be sent without warning into a deep trance state by predetermined command, or the dancer whose frenzied movements are induced automatically by a repetitious chant, the lover requires little else than an occasional exposure to continue his rapture. Many of us will recognize this account of a modern American adolescent infatuation:

I became attached to Mary but was much too shy to talk to her. In eighth grade, Mary came to my school. I kept a page in my notebook with the class, period, and teacher schedule for her and watched her whenever I could. Mary had a class right next to my science class, and I had fantasies of her coming over to my class for some reason, any reason. That year in science we studied VD, drugs, and the periodic table of elements. My stomach turned during VD and drugs and I got low grades, but the periodic table section of the class I got A's and was very excited, to give you an idea where my head was at. In ninth grade I had French 6th period. I got really low grades that year in French, and mostly thought about Mary being there (you know, "Gee what would it be like if she were here right now"; I even knew where she would sit because we were in alphabetical order) and about seeing up the dress of the girl that sat back of me about two seats in the next row. The next year I had to take French I over again and I had it first period. So did Mary. This year she really was in my class. I didn't need to imagine any more. Nothing turned out as great as my fantasies. The only time I talked with her was when I dropped my "moon ball" (it's like a whamo super ball, except it glows in the dark) and it rolled under her desk and she got it for me. I tried to think of cool ways to drop the ball again, but never thought of any.

His complicated feelings for Mary, simultaneously ridiculous and sublime, continued for more than six years, influencing his relationships with other girls, modifying all his other love experiences in that period of his life.

The ecstasy of infatuation is similar to other ecstasies in which human interaction is irrelevant, for the relationship part of falling in love is almost totally fantasized. It makes little difference that the contemplated object is human rather than wood or paint. The lover perceives the beloved as a fixed and immutable object, transcendent, a link to a higher state of existence or to an incomprehensible aspect of personal reality. The social mask of the beloved is replaced by a mythic mask in the eyes of the lover; the person behind the mask remains hidden and irrelevant.

The idealized passion of falling in love is not the only love experience of adolescence. Each way of uniting with another, infatuation, erotic attachment, and friendship, has its own ecstatic potential. What makes the adolescent's interactions so paradoxically humorous and heroic is that each facet of relating seems temporarily to exist in pure form. Each remains isolated from the other. For example, sexuality, the prime mover in the adolescent surge toward others, is almost always excluded (in fact if not in fantasy) from the experience of infatuation. The same adolescent may be passionately involved in a "Platonic" friendship and a relationship based purely on sex. A teenager might simultaneously swoon on hearing the voice of her idol, sleep with a boy her own age whose sexual needs she "puts up with" or perhaps exploits for sexual ends of her own, and be involved in an eternal tryst with her best girl friend. An anecdotal autobiography of an adult looking back on adolescence describes such a compartmentalization:

> When I was seventeen and a junior camp counselor, I was experiencing the joys of sex with a pretty counselor's helper whom I did not like, lusting after an unattainable girl whose thighs fed my masturbatory fantasies, and was involved in an intense friendship with a man which included occasional homosexual experiences. Each of these relationships touched deep chords inside of me. In retrospect, they seem tawdry, cheap, and unreal. But at the time, they were profound experiences that rivalled the religious and intellectual interests competing for my soul. Why couldn't I focus all of my passions on one person instead of spreading out the elements of myself so thinly among a variety of only partially acceptable lovers?

It is almost impossible to characterize adolescent love stories without reducing each experience to a category emphasizing incompleteness.

Another pattern of relationships during adolescence is based entirely on erotic attachment. Erotic feelings seem dramatically removed from childhood play or early social interactions. In adulthood we may realize that the quintessence of sex is derived from childhood and that social sensitivity is more importantly related to sexual "success" than phallus size or multi-orgasmic potential. But in adolescence, sexual development explodes into a new world where the past does not seem to apply. Adolescents are drawn inexorably toward experiencing sexual pleasures in relationships, but they feel unprepared to share their ecstatic feelings with others and to use relationships for anything other than dependency. And so at the beginning of puberty, the ecstatic potentials of sex are handled in secret, as earlier ecstatic feelings had been. Masturbation is isolated from the everyday world of relationships and the stab of orgasm is experienced only in the company of fantasies. The fantasies often become repetitive and plastic, as if to control the chaos of relationships in the adolescent's social world. Complex and anxiety-provoking interactions can be transformed into stereotypical images of fantasy. Sometimes these fantasies *seem* to become autonomous, particularly when they clash with conforming social roles. For example, homosexuals often describe their early erotic fantasies moving inevitably toward same-sexed situations as sexual excitement increased, no matter how they struggled against such a progression. But such fantasies rarely stay out of control for long. They may become disassociated from everyday interactions, but like a candle or mandala in other ecstatic inductions they become the stereotyped "fixed-point matrix" accompanying sexual pleasures.

It may take a long time for an adolescent to be ready to share his extraordinary sexual pleasures with a real Other. First attempts may take place in the secretive corner of a darkened movie theater or library. Social relationships which include petting may be carried on with pleading bravado when conquest and control are the issues; but orgasm itself may be faked or hidden so that the adolescent can avoid the risk of exposing truly uncontrollable pleasure with the Other. Even when open orgasm is finally achieved in the company of another, the individual may camouflage his desire in single-minded attraction to one part of his partner's body or to her clothing. Sexual attraction may depend on the size of breasts, the turn of a thigh, or muscular build rather than on a personal relationship. The extreme version of this situation is the so-called fetishist for whom all sexual attraction is focussed on an object which is distantly and obscurely related to the usual sources of sexual feeling. The derivation of a shoe or stocking fetish, or an irresistible desire for cats, pigs, or horses, can often be traced to a variety of childhood experiences. But the purpose served for the adolescent by these distortions is to subtract a small fixed element from the larger and more threatening matrix of human interaction. Even during intercourse, psychological merger can be attenuated by obscuring the sexual partner through fantasy—perhaps that identical to one used in masturbation.

Mythic symbols of the poignant separation of ecstatic sexual love from social relationships are common. Some come with a moral, like Beauty and the Beast, in which the girl is rewarded for loving the soul behind the ugly guise by having her beast turn out to be an enchanted prince. Cinderella, Donkey Skin, and countless other fairy tales rely on the fascination of the beauty and sexual joy that can lie hidden beneath an ugly garb.

The ancient myth of Eros and Psyche deals with this theme more explicitly. Psyche is a fifteen-year-old virgin who finds herself mysteriously alone and naked on an island. She discovers a house; inside is a bedroom that is totally dark. She goes to sleep there and is awakened in the night by someone in bed caressing her. In the darkness she does not at first understand what is happening. She thinks that the soft hands must be those of a woman; the hard object plunging into her a dragon. Gradually she realizes that her lover is a man. He comes each night and they have sexual encounters, although they rarely speak and she never sees him. At last she learns that he is the god Eros. She becomes increasingly curious to see him until, goaded by her jealous sister, she decides to risk it. She waits until he is asleep and lights a lamp, thus exposing the god's magnificent body. But a drop of oil spills from the lamp, burning Eros's penis. He immediately disappears and Psyche is doomed to search the earth for her lost lover. The myth is a classic odyssey of the movement from darkness toward self-discovery, one fraught with suffering for light and knowledge. In a scholarly afterword to his modern retelling of the tale, Michael Gall argues for the value of mature self-knowledge over infantilizing relationships, that is, of confrontation over passive acceptance of exquisite pleasures in the night.[9] Nevertheless, the journey from dark innocence is painful and removes Psyche forever from the naïve and purely erotic ecstasy that she enjoyed with her invisible lover. Once she has seen him, she can no longer lapse into total, innocent bliss.

It is the same basic tale for countless teenagers caught up in the early intoxication of physical pleasure. When the Other becomes corporeal, external, a real person, complications arise. As adolescent diaries emphasize again and again, the sensual and mystical levels of experience are closely intertwined. The psychological pattern of increasing sexual pleasure is similar to other "instant ecstasies." Sex, like amphetamines, drugs, strobe lights, and music, can bombard the sensations and overwhelm the ego until the ordinary modes of individual consciousness no longer include the experiential reality; more expanded, boundless states become manifest. Practical aspects of reality detract from this experience and make it more difficult to achieve.

The intense physical pleasures of orgasm with another is an experience which almost always goes beyond the "I" and the possibility of verbal description. Yet in the midst of caressing that leads to orgasm, there is also the awareness of other needs. The Other may add the magic dimension to sex that carries it beyond masturbation and toward the possibility of an ecstatic love relationship; but the Other may also inject a number of banal social conflicts that detract from the uncomplicated joys of pure erotic sex.

Interpersonal difficulties are not easily isolated from the physical relationship; they find their way into the sexual encounter itself. Working out day-to-day relationships, as one would with a commitment to a deepening friendship, is more urgent and therefore more difficult when sexual pleasures are also at stake. As a relationship becomes complex it becomes more difficult to give oneself up to the experience. Instead the observing "I's" stay active; sex is made part of relationship games instead of freeing the two selves from their social masks. The girl is afraid to get on top of the boy even if she finds it sexually satisfying because she might express an unacceptable aggressiveness; or perhaps she is afraid to have an orgasm while underneath him for fear of becoming submissive. The boy may feel he has to concentrate on *her* orgasm rather than on their mutual pleasure because he does not want to seem insensitive to her needs; or he may feel compelled to keep thrusting to the point of boredom rather than risk being thought unable to satisfy her or keep an erection. She may want to make him feel inadequate more than she wants the pleasure of an orgasm and sensual involvement and thus she holds back. He may want her to feel used and so be rough and inconsiderate. The games have endless variations, but they always reflect an aspect of the social relationship. Sometimes they expose unacknowledged feelings of one partner for the other and give the first hint of a minor dissatisfaction in the relationship. Adolescent sex is often more pleasurable with less rather than more interpersonal intimacy, for it is impossible to idealize the Other once the personal intimacies surrounding sex are included in a relationship. The couple may learn to come together for sex alone or use social groups to buffer their relationship rather than try to work out a friendship together.

Friendship is yet another prominent pattern of relationship in the panoply of adolescent love. As adults we may take it for granted or confuse our relationships with acquaintances for friendships. Friendship is a part of our network of alliances; its pleasures are often rationalized by its social advantages. The more intimate the friendship, the greater the tendency to add further dimensions to the relationship. In a heterosexual orientation, friendship between men and women presses toward sexual discovery, between two men or two women toward the adoption of some common cause, sport, or business deal, if sexual behavior is taboo (or gratified elsewhere). The question of sexual union may arise in same-sex friendships when friends wonder if it would add a beneficial level of communication and fulfillment to the relationship.

C. S. Lewis says of friendship that it is

> the least *natural* of loves; the least instinctive, organic, biological, gregarious and necessary. I have no duty to be anyone's friend and no man in the world has a duty to be mine. No claims, no shadow of

necessity. Friendship is unnecessary, like philosophy, like art, like the universe itself. It has no survival value, rather it is one of those things which give value to survival.[10]

Because it is the least necessary for our survival, to our breeding, or to the raising of our children, its emotional peaks are more rarefied, belonging to the "luminous, tranquil, rational world of real relationships freely chosen." For Lewis, friendship seems to raise on "to the level of the gods or angels." Part of its sublimity can lie in the fact that the awkward moments of sexual intimacy, the intense peaks and gratifications of need, do not detract from the more mellow plateau of joy.

Friends do not "fall in love." They do not remain personally mysterious to one another. Nor do they rely on sexual caresses or erotic experience. And yet all the elements necessary for ecstatic experience are present in friendship. In Lewis's phrase: "Eros will have naked bodies; friendship naked personalities." It begins with the same painful, awkward gestures that characterize physical lovers. The social conventions are exaggerated, explored, and finally discarded as more and more intimate disclosures are allowed. In a sense sexual disrobing is a far simpler process because the potential for pleasure is so clear and the anatomical end point so specific. The joys of friendship are contained in the gradually increasing pleasure of sharing secrets and reciprocating trust. Knowing another human being, his psychological workings, his emotions, his prejudices, his thoughts, begins out of curiosity but soon progresses toward a more ultimate form of knowing. The bond of friendship becomes ecstatic when intimacy and personal knowledge reach out beyond the social games of personal disclosure and confession, beyond a common purpose, until all boundaries dissolve and the oneness of humanity, represented in the oneness of the friends, becomes the core experience.

Erik Erikson defines the central developmental task of adolescence as identity formation and reserves the possibility of intimacy, the true condition for love relationships, as a post-adolescent phenomenon. Writing of heterosexual friendship he says:

> There is a kind of adolescent attachment between boy and girl which is often mistaken either for mere sexual attraction or for love. Except where the mores demand heterosexual behavior, such attachment is often devoted to an attempt at arriving at a definition of one's identity by talking things over endlessly, by confessing what one feels like and what the other seems like, and by discussing plans, wishes, expectations.[11]

The ecstasies of adolescent friendship are as immediate, sporadic, and fickle as other adolescent loves. Relationships are rapidly established on very few clues of mutuality, but they are just as rapidly dissolved if the clues prove false. As each layer of self is exposed, each participant must choose whether or not to incorporate what has been revealed as part of the relationship. When areas of disagreement are uncovered, the pair must choose between the barriers of deceit and unspoken disapproval and the discomfort of fighting through to a mutual sensitivity to irreconcilable differences. Friends do not have to agree about everything; they simply have to respect and trust each other and be willing to struggle to understand and accept those things which they may not particularly like.

There is a dyadic duet in friendship that mirrors the movement of bodies during sexual intercourse; trusting, merger with the other, is followed by pulling away in fear that one's self might be swallowed and lost. A young woman of nineteen describes that feeling as she wrestles with a deepening friendship:

> I love Suzie and want to be close to her. It's not a sexual thing, but a wanting to really be close to someone, to really know them. But each time I move toward knowing her, I feel that I will dissolve into her and that I will be lost.

When asked if that frightened or excited her, she replied, "I really want that to happen. But I don't want to know the worst about myself and her. And I don't want to lose myself and wake up her."

A married woman in her early twenties described her first encounter with her former childhood and teenage best friend since they had both been married:

> The men had left the room briefly, so we were alone together. She was relating to me as a more experienced woman because I'd had a baby and she hadn't. She asked about breast feeding and whether it ruined a woman's figure. I listened and heard old themes from the past—her early development; my flat-chested years; our endless discussions of boys and what girls should or shouldn't do with them; our getting mistaken for each other because we were the same height and wore our hair the same; our double dating and choosing boy friends who knew each other—and suddenly I felt myself tip forward, almost in a swoon. With the dizziness came a rush of passion, a need not to kiss her, but to enter into her through her mouth, to fall inside her being. She looked at me, at first with concern, then with fear and horror as she thought I was leaning forward to kiss her on the lips. Wide-eyed, she shouted my name. I withdrew, as though she had slapped me. I've never understood what it meant, but I've never forgotten that moment. If it was homosexual lust, it was strangely unerotic . . .

This is the dramatic fear of all merger experience, the possibility of death and rebirth that the gurus of every tradition warn must be experienced to be transcended. Eventually beyond that barrier there is the possibility of the paring away of all protective layers until the other's thoughts and feelings are trustfully shared.

The social skills necessary to engage in such a quest are complex and above all require courage to face the mutual revelations that are its by-products. To some extent the development of a friendship has immediate roots in childhood social experience. Unlike sexual encounters in adolescence (which seem so new and whose root skills are derived from the earliest infant sensualities) the skills of adolescent friendship appear to be much more continuously derived from social relationships of latency.

Adolescents have been involved in developing social skills ever since the line between self and other was first tentatively drawn in childhood. As brothers or sisters in a close family they experienced an intimacy which, though a result of the circumstances of birth, may nonetheless have provided the knowledge of another human being that presages the ecstatic friendships of adolescence. Because the joys of intimacy with a few select companions are already part of their personal experience, adolescents can feel that they are building on familiar ground as they develop new relational skills. And unlike the seemingly irrational basis on which the choice of sexual objects is determined, they may choose friends with the wish to by-pass difference and conflict. They may proceed more warily and less passionately to establish a firm base from which to take a further leap into ecstatic merger.

Perhaps that is why the friendships made in adolescence tend to outlast the more tumultuous infatuations and sexual affairs which occur during the same period of time. Yet the price for such durability is the same fragmentation that was evident in the other ecstatic relationships. Time and again, strong friendships disintegrate when sexuality appears. Erotic encounters tend too often to become an end that precludes other activities altogether. The same is often true if "hero worship" becomes too critical an element in the friendship. Yet of all the ecstatic relationships common in adolescence, friendship comes closest to requiring the training and effort that characterize a continuing quest for ecstasy. The participants in a friendship may intermittently withdraw from the profound encounter and still maintain skills necessary to support a renewed encounter. Unlike infatuation or the distracting intensity of erotic attachment, friendship can continue on a superficial level until its more profound aspects re-emerge perhaps months or years later.

Separating the varieties of love experiences into distinct relationships simplifies the feelings of confusion that each new interaction generates in the adolescent. Each encounter feels excitingly fresh to the intellect, emotions, and senses. New love may be a weekly event. There is a hunger for passionate closeness on every dimension of human interaction, yet the various dimensions are kept separate from one another. A youth may swear eternal union and practice rampant infidelity. It is as if relationships are dissected into their component parts and each element is then plumbed to its ecstatic depths as an experience of love.

As adolescence progresses, however, the separation of these elements may seem limiting. At first it is enough to enjoy the wonder of the different love experiences. Each is a complete route in itself to the core experience of merger with another. The various archetypes of young love portrayed by Dante and Beatrice, Eros and Psyche, David and Jonathan, and all their modern counterparts are not perceived as lesser experiences. The love expressed in each of these myths is complete in itself. Yet there is also an inexorable movement toward unity and wholeness in the ecstatic consciousness. More is required in each relationship. Nothing must be held back when the love experience is explored. It is like a monk increasing the time of his fast, like Bal Shem Tov praying for nights and days to pierce the heaven with his cries, like the acid worshipper increasing the micrograms of chemical until he can span all time and space. In love as in all ecstatic journeys, the union strives to become total. Friendship and sexuality cannot be separated from each other indefinitely, nor can infatuation remain free from erotic and interpersonal intimacy. With more time and experience, the adolescent's quest for love attempts to encompass all the elements of ecstatic relationship in one lover.

The goal of finding one other person and one love relationship gradually becomes a central focus for most adolescents. The search has its roots in the archaic knowledge of ecstatic consciousness, in the surety that such a person and relationship once fulfilled transcendent needs. Unfortunately, it is rare for one adolescent relationship to hold out the promise of ecstatic union to its participants for very long. Without giving up the ideal, late adolescents and young adults find that friends are separated from lovers, lovers from idols. Long-term relationships may become non-ecstatic liaisons. As in latency, late adolescents often experience intermittent ecstasy in solitude through non-relational traditions. Even when the sexual reflex is integrated into relationships, physical joy may be peripheral or pleasurable only when fantasy predominates or when the affair is isolated from the day-to-day world. Relationships which feed the need for security rather than ecstatic love may be used but devalued. The real partner may increasingly be held in contempt while the ideal is made ever more exotic and magical.

For some adolescents whose ecstatic orientation has already been shaped in another direction than the dyad, the challenge of integrating ecstasy and relational needs is too difficult. They may seek paths which offer the same experiential rewards without the complications arising from another intervening and changeable person. Dyadic ecstasy in continuing love relationships may feel like a mirage. Solitary and group modes may be more attainable. This splitting of relational dynamics and the ecstatic quest, which often draws support from similar childhood patterns, may continue into adulthood and shape the quality and expectations of marriage.

There is a sense in which adolescence represents a unique nodal point in both the development of love relationships and the focussing of ecstatic experience. Unlike the child, whose choices were limited by sexual immaturity and social immobility, the adolescent has a full range of capabilities which can be employed in defining himself and his relationships to others. The actual choices open to him are dramatically increased in both his own and society's eyes. Nevertheless, the important family relationships of childhood will have already placed limits and directions on his ecstatic orientation. By the time of puberty some children are already strongly inhibited from expressing strong emotions in the presence of their mother, father, or siblings. Others will have learned to move toward people only under the protection of their fantasies. Still others may have begun to sever the connection between relationships and ecstatic feelings in favor of a more controllable focus for their pleasures.

Adolescent love relationships are developed in the sacred space and time that accompanies a special rite of passage; it is free from the ordinary boundaries of profane existence. It becomes increasingly difficult to carry these relationships beyond their initial stages and to combine their many aspects into a meaningful unity as the end of the developmental stage is reached. The demands of society pressure young adults toward compromising the productless world of ecstatic experience. The commitment to a continuing quest for a love relationship is based on a fragmented glimpse of what might be possible. It rarely can compete with the practical demands of adult survival. The ecstatic quest in the dyad may die out as the need for "adjustment" increases. The patterns of ecstatic relationship that have been part of the adolescent world are frequently regularized into more stable and dependable packages which have society's stamp of approval and do not interfere with the need to make a living and provide for a family.

No matter how thoroughly the adult world obscures the past, the glimpse of nirvana in another's eyes remains a memory, a romantic fantasy. No matter how "workable" a marriage or other relationship, if it lacks ecstasy this absence will be felt. Ecstatic consciousness begins in the pre-relational world of symbiotic merger. That potential is present in all human encounters. Socially functional interactions based on lesser visions will always feel incomplete. The adult may spend his life trying to reconcile the split between his style of living and his idealized love of adolescence. Social and psychological maturity bring no guarantee that the individual will experience transcendent union in love.

7

Adult Love

YOUNG adults share with toddlers the breathtaking possibilities of a fresh start. All forms of living and loving seem practical and possible. They have the freedom to choose anew their styles of relating and their ecstatic pursuits, to establish a family on their own terms or stay free from dependent relationships, to belong to a familiar group or form a bond that has no ties with the past. In this energetic thrust toward a new life, most young adults accept the dyad as the predominant relationship form. Love is pursued for its ecstatic possibilities. Sex and profound relating are always felt to be on the verge of happening if they are not being experienced at the moment. Without the extended family or community to cushion the loneliness of solitary living, young adults passionately seek one another's company with the exhilarating expectation of sharing a continuously ecstatic and meaningful life free from the mistakes of the past.

In fact, the pairings of young adulthood are not necessarily ecstatic. Adults may appear to be free, but they also have powerful constraints on their freedom. They may recognize external factors such as social and economic pressures that keep them back from their idealized goals; they are less likely to see the limits imposed by their own psychological needs. Adolescents were free to experiment because they had the continuing security provided by parents and peers. Adults have less support. They have ingrained patterns based on their original merger experience of pre-relational days and on the ecstatic and relational forms developed during childhood and adolescence. Many paths "freely" chosen by young adults lead back to these patterns, namely, to long-standing conflicts between dependency needs and ecstatic orientation. The new life rarely breaks free from old ways even when it rejects former relationships and places. The course of adult love is at every stage controlled by the tension between the flight from isolation in the search for dependence and the flight from dependence in the search for ecstasy.

Ecstasy in adulthood need not be limited to dyadic experience any more than successful marriage has to include ecstatic experience. Adult *love,* however, requires merger in a dyad, whether in a brief affair, in a series of limited relationships, or in a long-term commitment. It is this extended commitment in a love relationship that is most like other ecstatic traditions. Like them it is a remarkable rather than an ordinary occurrence. Above all it requires a single-minded devotion to a way of life. It is important to realize that such devotion is only one way to handle a relationship, not necessarily the best way for everyone. In each relationship the "fit" of the couple and their changing interaction with one another will provide the raw material for an unfolding process in which ecstatic life and relational life are continually changing. Individuals with a solitary orientation may need a secure relationship as a necessary support in order to embark on separate quests. For them the dyad may at times provide its own ecstatic potential, but its primary task is as a home base for solitary ventures. On the other hand, individuals oriented to the group may experience the dyadic relationship as a necessary developmental bridge to the family or to larger social groupings. Couples in which both partners are most excited by the dyadic mode will find greatest meaning in working toward ongoing ecstatic love with a single Other.

Even for those oriented to love as their ecstatic way, fantasy expectations and reality relationships may not match. Repeated discouragement is almost inevitable. Perhaps the most malignant temptations are the doubts that failure brings, the lingering possibility that the longed-for dyadic merger in a real relationship is an illusion. It is extremely difficult to trust an inner expectation when outside relationships of one's own and one's friends seem so fragile and society offers so many other ways. Discouraged and doubtful, many turn away from the search for a long-term love relationship toward other modes of experience only to find that they are unsatisfying and meaningless. Some blame their lack of success on not finding the right person; others on social incompetence or failure in other areas of their lives such as work; still others on political and social conditions. These may be accurate perceptions of events. The right person, a sense of individual security and competence, and supportive social conditions may all play important roles in being able to continue in a very difficult struggle toward relationship. But there are also doubts which undermine the commitment to the dyad and the love tradition and which may cover up deep-seated fears of a personal inability to love or an unwillingness to face the aspects of self that might be uncovered in a totally open relationship. The same temptations of disbelief, impatience, and compromise prey on those who seek ecstasy in love relationships as in all other ecstatic traditions. In love even more than in other Ways, personal needs must be confronted.

A commitment to the love tradition begins in the acceptance of struggle. Particularly for the young adult it is often extremely difficult to appreciate how complex the process will become. Many are trapped in patterns forced on them by childhood experience and use a myth such as a rescue fantasy to structure their relationships. A man may see himself as a "knight in shining armor" in search of a maiden to rescue from an ogre. When he finds himself behaving in an unheroic way or feels the woman moving outside her role, he may flee from the relationship and seek another "damsel in distress." It is not uncommon for women who have lost their fathers at an early age constantly to seek out new men, looking for an ecstatic union with a mysterious stranger. They may become call girls or entertainers, always anticipating a magical encounter that never happens. With a well-structured fantasy, the other people are not real but are satisfactory only as they fulfill their predetermined roles. Intermittent encounters with persons who partially fulfill the dream may keep an unrealistic hope alive.

Men and women in their late twenties are often trapped by a dream based on childhood needs, nurtured through the romantic love culture of true-confession magazines or the sex-and-dating ethic of *Playboy*, and maintained by current psychological needs. As they move through successive affairs, repetitive dates and disappointments, infatuations and near misses, they may begin to perceive the gap between fantasy and reality. The people they go out with may increasingly fall into stereotypes. There are the "safe" but unexciting relationships which die slowly from lack of passion. Quite separate from these are tainted, short-lived, but wildly erotic relationships which are carefully isolated from day-to-day living. A man may find himself perpetually returning to women he cannot respect because he is unable to resolve his desire for an ecstatic sexual encounter with the desire for a comfortable, dependent relationship. Even if the woman is capable of a healthy relationship, the man can see her only in his original stereotype. This split between the safe and the exciting is easy to reconcile with marriage, which can become a "safe" compartment while extramarital encounters provide the excitement. While this pattern is most commonly associated with men—the salesman who leaves the wife with the kids and has a "loose" woman in each town, or the judge who keeps his family for his social position and his mistress for excitement—it is also common among women. A woman may bring home comfortable dates that get along well with her family but are physically unattractive to her; then she may have "flings" in which she goes to a bar to pick up (or let herself be picked up by) a man who does not "respect" her and with whom she can have an exciting sexual encounter disassociated from the rest of her life. To get beyond such limited stereotyping takes the courage to encounter the Other and embrace more than a dream; to open oneself to the uncontrollable variety of a total person who is both safe and exciting, who sees one as both strong and weak. It may take years of experimental half-relationships before an adult can find one Other with whom to entrust all aspects of self and "I."

Occasionally two individuals will form a profound ecstatic bond that is based more on interlocking fantasies than on real encounter. Such relationships may become long-term in spite of their practical difficulties. The lovers are plagued by the conflict between ecstatic experience and interpersonal needs. These are the tempestuous love affairs that feed the agonized delights of movie-goers and novel readers, for whom relationships are modelled upon the romantic myths of Tristan and Isolde or Scarlet O'Hara and Rhett Butler. The members project each other into dramatic roles but never achieve person-to-person communication. Such relationships frequently thrive on intense beginnings and endings but have no middle. There may be frequent fights, desperate jealousies, accusations. The gulf between them is more than simply a lack of social skills which may be solved by better communication. Instead it springs from a discordance nourished by fantasies which cannot be realized in the relationship. Security is traded for passion. Couples want to love each other but cannot live together. They cannot depend on one another or do anything for the other's existential loneliness except in the brief moments of the ecstatic experience itself. Yet they do move beyond the practicalities of relating to the other reality whose roots extend back to the archetypal merger potentials of earliest childhood.

Adults frozen within such chaotic liaisons are often driven by intense emotions that were established in their earliest love encounters, which often centered around feelings of both love and hate toward a romanticized, absent, or lost member of the family. The roots of the enveloping passion may remain obscure and surface only as a symbol of the past hidden in an irresistible physical or psychological quality of the partner.

We all share an individual past with many kinds of losses. The attempt to recapture and regain, in however disguised and symbolic a form, will motivate every decision in our lives. In terms of development of an ecstatic consciousness, we share the common heritage of having lost the symbiotic merger states of early infancy in the process of developing a sense of individuality. If the individual who is trapped in an impossible fantasy or who is linked in an intense love-hate relationship is different from the rest of us, it is only in the all-consuming nature of his focus on recapturing the sense of union with another even at the expense of comfortable adjustment. All of us are capable of such unbalanced patterns. We may be unwilling to take the risk of passionate caring or we may have found a healthy way to integrate our passion into our daily lives. We may feel superior to neurotic lovers who are stuck in the need to correct an unfortunate past, but we can also see that they are caught up in the breathtaking emotions of the experience of regaining a fantasy world more real than reality. We may be glad that we are not seized by the destructive passions of Romeo and Juliet, but we thrill to the vicarious pleasure of hearing their story. "It is better to have loved and lost than never to have loved at all." In psychological terms this means, "It is better to risk experimenting openly with relationships than staying inside the safe shell of the 'I.' "

Young adulthood begins with two very different interpersonal challenges. The first is the sudden possibility of developing a *real* ongoing relationship which fulfills the common fantasies of adolescents. The second is finding meaningful social relationships to replace the loss of security from the family group. The complexities of individual history heavily determine the kinds of initial choices made in balancing ecstatic experience with security needs within relationships. Persons for whom dyadic ecstasy is unimportant may be able to feel at ease with superficial relationships while searching for socially appropriate mates or enjoying the sexual freedom of the young adult culture. On the other hand, persons with a strong dyadic orientation may have a series of tumultuous affairs as they discover their real relationships are less ecstatic than their fantasy encounters. They may find that most individuals either do not fulfill or do not reciprocate their fantasies. Even if they find the kind of willing, magical person they seek, the relationship may flounder on their lack of requisite social skills to bind themselves into a workable union. To take up the process of a long-term ecstatic bond, both partners must continually modulate their perception of the Other while accepting fluctuations in the experience and flaws in the idea, that is, while risking the alterations of "I" that come from merger with a real "You." The relationship must be stable and communicative enough and satisfy enough dependency needs that the irrational angers and estrangements which are part of learning to know and merge with someone in the deepest sense do not destroy the possibility of continuing to be together.

If two individuals fall in love who are both oriented to the dyadic experience as their basic ecstatic mode, they search for ways to continue their merger experience as a sexual encounter, as a profound friendship, as an archetypal union. Their initial tendency may be to wall off their union from the profanity of day-to-day events much as adolescents hide their loves in secret fantasies or monks retreat to solitary cells. A long honeymoon or the trend toward "living together" are short-term institutionalized equivalents of the need for a couple to be alone together. But adult love, if it is to persist, must wrestle with the same demons as the other ecstatic traditions. It must deal with external demands and cope with the business of a daily routine. It must compete with other interests, other loves, other merger experiences in the lives of its partners.

To remain committed to such an intense experience with the Other often seems an insurmountable task even when the relationship is experimental in the sense that no long-term social commitment has been undertaken. As in most ecstatic ways, there is a multitude of techniques which may be extremely useful in pursuing the path. Exercises in sensuality, sexual and communicative games, relational strategies, may all be important enriching procedures which help two individuals to explore and deepen their union much as special techniques for prayer or meditation aid in other ecstatic traditions. Yet mastery of any given technique may also serve to obscure and change the more important processes. Devotion to a technique may be used as a way to escape the relationship rather than develop it. In the case of the love tradition, one or the other of the partners may grasp sex or massage as the ultimate experience much as seekers in the yogic tradition may lose themselves in the excesses of bodily control or mental power. Or there may be a frenetic search for newer and more radical ways to explore one another, much as addicts of "instant" ecstasies may float from one meditative system or mind-altering drug to another. The balance between techniques as enrichment and as escape is quite delicate. Often those who submerge themselves in a technical quest for a better way reflect an uneasiness about their commitment to the union itself and a lessening of confidence in their ability to have a love relationship without mechanical props. They are working on details rather than perceiving the larger pattern.

Marriage (or its equivalent forms) usually implies a commitment to the formation of a new unit. This new unit might be the embryo of a long-term love relationship in the sense we have defined it here. The guiding ecstatic form of such a *dyadically oriented marriage would be a commitment to the two-person merger rather than to each of the individuals or to the family group.* Individual growth and development would be in the service of enriching this merger rather than the separate self and the "I." The family too would primarily be seen as enriching the parental couple and only secondarily in providing a group merger experience. If merger rather than individuality is the common goal, then every event would become imbued with meaning for the shared consciousness. Such a relationship can use the crises of the life cycle—pregnancy, birth, and illness—as sacred ceremonies for celebrating a renewed union. Every daily act may also hold the potential for transforming two-person interactions into fusion. Any couple that wants to stay together in an intense relationship must work continually to establish and maintain the nature and meaning of their particular dyad.

There are other concepts than ecstatic merger with which to organize a marriage. One well-defined alternative is an *individually oriented marriage* (the so-called open marriage) in which the living structure is designed to maintain the "I" rather than foster dissolution. *Separateness and individuality are maximized at the expense of merger and union.* Roles, however liberated, are also kept precise. Separate work identities and social and sexual relationships emphasize the lack of restriction on each individual's explorations. It is not an easy commitment to maintain. Intimate daily living has a way of leading beyond roles toward a more engrossing merger; and sexual relationships begun as a way of exploring new sensations tend toward more enmeshed social relationships and their consequences. Nevertheless, individually oriented marriage is an important alternative for those who need a secure relationship to draw upon, but whose primary ecstatic path is solitary.

Another alternative is a *group or family-oriented marriage* in which the couple's initial union comes to be submerged in a form which *is oriented toward a collective merger rather than toward each individual or the dyad.* At first this may be realized in a marriage that is barely a more formalized extension of the earlier pairings within a teenage gang. The same friends are maintained and meaningful occasions are shared by the group while the couple's union is experienced as of secondary importance. With the coming of children, the family unit takes over as the most important experience and parental roles and relationships provide a common interest with other families. The dyad lives only through such developing group forms. Societies tend to support this way since it reinforces marriage's function to propagate the species. It also settles potentially disruptive lovers into solid citizens working to build a clan or a community. Yet it can de-emphasize the individual's other goals, particularly those of ecstatic experience in a dyadic form.

The contract of a dyadic marriage is radical and demanding. It supports neither individual self-realization within the marriage nor parental function and child-raising. Many if not most couples begin with a passionate urge for union, but few sustain the intense dyadic form. In the primary creation myth of our culture and the allegorical model for our marriages, Adam and Eve began their relationship in a union. Eve was taken from Adam's body and made into an extension of his own being. Adam and Eve soon began to differentiate themselves from each other. Instead of sharing in the work of preserving the blissful dyad in Eden, Eve listened to the serpent and ate the forbidden fruit. With the knowledge of good and evil came the self-conscious awareness of differences. Discovering two separate selves, they clothed their strange bodies and traded the ongoing union of paradise for intermittent sexual passion. While Adam and Eve remained loyal mates after their banishment, they could not again enjoy unconflicting pleasures. Lovers may strive for union without conflict, but when the reality of worldly existence, the knowledge of good and evil, descends upon them, they look at each other in a new way and set about the "serious" business of marriage and raising a family. Or so our myth implies.

The story of Adam and Eve is a metaphor for a valid form of marital adjustment, the shifting of a relationship from merger to individual discovery and eventually to group and family living in order to remain in harmony with the biological life cycle. Many couples re-enact the myth. They begin with a sense of total union, entering marriage with an idealistic belief in the ecstatic potential of sharing a life, a social identity, a name and address. There may be a slow realization that whatever the spouse does is reflected on one's own identity and that union brings constraints as well as a sense of completion. It is not unusual to find a young man or woman who is filled with distrust and even contempt for the person he had adored just a few weeks or months before. When Cupid's blindfold falls from their eyes, the partners in the dyad suddenly see that their relationship has a different and perhaps less romantic meaning than they had supposed. With the realization that merger has been taking place on pragmatic as well as idealistic levels comes the horror that the Other is impossible to control, like the self off sleep-walking, behaving unpredictably yet reflecting one's own nature and status.

For our current fluid life styles it has been suggested that all intense lovers should have three or four mates during their life time. The first mate would be suited to the rapture of falling in love, to adolescent intensity. The second would be more practical and supportive, the social anchor of a growing family unit. A third would make a stimulating companion in the freer life style after children are grown and traditional sex-role divisions harder to justify. The last mate would be someone suited to mystic retreat and transcendent reunion as life ebbed away and death became a more immediate concern. This suggests institutionalized serial polygamy or renewal through creating new dyads and thereby essentially new life. In practice many men and women reach middle age already having had two or three legal mates. Success, however, requires more than a new mate. If the quest is toward living together in ecstasy, it requires using adult social skills to integrate the fragmenting tendencies of adolescent love. It requires discipline and the ability to discover *renewal* within the ecstatic potential of the Other.

Renewal can be found in many forms, some integral to our biological nature, others external or societal. Sex, life crises, parenting, social experimentation, religion, and death may all have their impact on the dyad, either to renew or destroy, depending upon how they are used.

Sex is our biology's ultimate self-renewing pleasure; its joys are pivotal to all dyadic ecstasy, but especially to long-term experience. It is always a merger experience if just for the physical union that takes place when male and female interpenetrate. But even more profoundly, the term is appropriate because of the experience of spiritual or psychological union that frequently occurs during orgasm. We use such words as "dissolve," "melt," "fall," "sink," or "fuse" when trying to convey the moment but know that it is an experience beyond words, though one which often leaves us with a sense that we briefly possessed something that now escapes us. Orgasm can be and often is experienced as a loss of ego boundaries, a union with a god-like principle, a participation in the rhythms of universal life. A follower of Wilhelm Reich describes the experience of sexual intercourse as the pinnacle of ecstatic experience and the epitome of psychological health:

> When the unarmored person is able to surrender totally with mind and body, without fantasies or reservations, to the partner and the sexual experience. When this happens, the total orgasm is involved, with nothing held back. It is the most transcendent experience possible in life. At the apex of the act when the union is complete the two separate energy fields merge and become one, the partners feel a unity with the entire universe.[1]

Sex does not necessarily reach such heights. The nature of the union will be critical, for only in a love relationship in which "we" rather than "I" is sought can the experience reach such totality. In marriages based on dependency, sex might be handled as a routine release of tension affording only transitory pleasure. In marriages which emphasize individuality, ecstatic sex involving psychological as well as physical merger must eventually be excluded to avoid the threat of getting lost in the Other. Private fantasies can be used to maintain the personal boundary and deny the partner at the moment of orgasm. In group-oriented marriages, dyadic ecstasy also threatens rather than strengthens the basic premise of the union. Sex between the couple may be routinized while group settings or temporary couplings are used as a "safe" place for more ecstatic experience.

For two individuals (heterosexual or homosexual) committed totally to the love tradition and the path of merger, *sex will become their celebration of reunion* much as a long fast or ritual drug experience may provide a periodic resacralizing experience in other traditions. The comfort of non-verbal physical contact reflects acceptance of the Other at the most primitive levels. In the honesty of physical encounter, half-hidden restraints and involuntary distancing maneuvers can be worked through with extraordinary simplicity. Arguments cannot be resolved by sex alone, but the total interaction of naked bodies and shared souls is an intimate way to reach understanding of the Other. This state is reflected in the biblical use of the verb "to know" instead of "to copulate." At its best, shared sexual experience can provide not only a frequent revitalization of ecstasy in merger but also a reification of the sense of transcendence and transpersonal experience that is sought in a true dyadic love relationship.

With the possible exception of sex, most of the potent sources of renewal for relationships are linked directly to life-cycle changes. Like sex, their power comes from their tendency to create new merger experiences, new ecstatic moments which, temporarily at least, transcend the old patterns and the old ways. Adults rarely think of life-cycle changes as altering their patterns of relating, for such changes are not as dramatic as the radical endocrine shifts in puberty which alter adolescent relationships. Yet the rites of passage which order society are symbolic of real changes in relational patterns that occur as life progresses. Marriage, birth, and death are the most conspicuous, particularly because they are surrounded by rituals even in our secular culture. Pregnancy and menopause both provide hormonal changes as radical as those of adolescence and provide new roles and alter relational needs. Illness and old age too may transform the body into states that are virtually discontinuous with the individual's concept of who he is and the way others relate to him.

Change is further marked by events in the lives of parents and children. Adults are so intimately linked to their extended family that they experience profound changes in their own identities around key moments in family life. A mother dies, a son graduates from school, a father has a heart attack, a daughter marries—and the son/father and the daughter/mother move into a period of personal chaos to emerge with an altered concept of who they are and how to relate with others. Thus for adulthood as for earlier stages, there is both continuity with the past and disruption. These changes radically affect the desire for ecstatic experience and the quality of relationships; and they also affect the sense of aloneness or relationship and feelings of competence or dependence.

It is far more complicated to trace the adult love cycle than to show the typical progress of earlier stages of development. The consistent human patterns of growth and change become increasingly variable. Illness, aging, and death are inevitable, but their timing is less predictable than puberty or the beginnings of speech. Adults may not be free from parental supervision until after they are parents themselves; or they may find themselves without parents before they have formed an adult bond. The timing of such factors may be controlled by chance or desire and have an extreme influence on relational needs. Marriage, pregnancy, and family life are transition points of enormous importance, but they are far from inevitable in today's social climate. They may occur at any time from sixteen to sixty, either once, recurrently, or not at all, for they are determined by social choice as much as by biological rhythm.

The beginning of a family is the most obvious example of a life-cycle change with the potential for totally disrupting an ongoing union despite an intense effort by a couple to remain on a dyadic course. The practical demands of family life diminish or even preclude the growth of the dyad's ecstatic potential. The intrusion of in-laws may remind the partners of their separate origins and attachments and strain their sense of union. With the advent of children, the experience of merger with the family group may overshadow or obviate the separate existence of the dyad.

In "The Symposium," the wise woman Diotima explains the relationship between love and generation to Socrates. "Marvel not then at the love which all men have of their offspring; for that universal love and interest is for the sake of immortality." [2] Only through generation, she maintains, can the mortal partake of immortality. Although a couple may be motivated by profound and universal biological urges toward ecstatic union, their choice to have children forces the dyad to incorporate new elements within its boundaries. It stimulates profound transformations in the individuals and places the primal unit within a larger whole as only one dyad within a larger configuration which includes other dyadic possibilities. And yet children symbolize the union of man and woman on a most profound level. A baby is an objective sign of sexual union. It also represents the biological merger of the two genetic pools. The nurture of the child depends on economic and social cooperation. The child will ultimately combine psychological factors absorbed from the two parents as a single reality.

Conception represents joint participation in a fundamental miracle of creation. Merger is not only with the other parent, but also with the baby, who is literally an extension of one's own being. Most people are thrilled and excited by pregnancy, by watching a particle of self transform into an Other. Yet even as parents grasp the glory of creating a new being, they may tremble at the intimacy and intrusion of this new creature on their unconscious emotions and feel threatened by the new pressures it exerts on the boundaries of the dyad.

The threat is real, for these life transitions do destroy as well as enrich. Couples committed to an individually oriented marriage or to a profound dyad may deal with the threat of family by choosing not to have children. For the individually oriented marriage, a family may signify more shared commitments, parental sex-role divisions, and less individual freedom—in short, the possibility of the destruction of a workable life style in return for a new kind of union with a new level of risks. For the couple committed to the dyad, children and family life offer a similar threat—a movement away from each other and toward a different kind of merger experience which could either destroy or transcend their own.

Yet a couple pursuing their love relationship cannot simply close off further life experience and hope to capture the present. The decision to limit what is possible between two people, even when taken out of positive motives, often turns out to restrict more than enhance. In fact there is no way to lock out intrusions or keep an individual involved in a relationship by decreasing an important element of his nature. The challenge for the lovers is how to share each new experience so that the relationship is expanded and deepened without either partner losing touch with the basic commitment to one another in the shared venture.

New parents will inevitably experience change in their individual and dyadic identities. There will be new strains on the relationship as the basic assumptions of parenting are awakened in each—expectations formed in early childhood before they met their mates. Suddenly the good lover or spouse may seem an inappropriate father or mother. Sex-linked roles tend to become more pronounced. The couple may struggle to retain a sense that even while performing separate functions they form a single part of a meaningful total pattern. The parent/child dyad may threaten to become more ecstatic than the husband/wife dyad. A mother may turn toward other women for security and the confirmation of her role, while her predominant pleasure and ecstatic participation is in the primal act of motherhood. A husband may turn toward work or to a solitary orientation, finding nothing ecstatic in the new family group or in his transformed woman. Pregnancy and childbirth introduce a massive change in the marital arrangement. The husband/wife dyad may experience profound renewal together; they may merge into a larger unit such as the family; or they may split apart into separated patterns of ecstatic experience.

The conflict between the opposing forces of dissolution or renewal of the primal ecstatic pair that begins during pregnancy and childbirth continues through the entire parenting process. In the past, and in more traditional societies, the ecstatic potential and bonds of security between parent and child may outweigh the importance of the marital union; marriage served procreative rather than relational needs. More recently, parenting and even mothering have become socially devalued while sexual freedom and coupling have been given much positive value. A family may threaten the dyadic union because of its lack of meaning rather than because of its power and importance in the culture.

Yet even today many couples find that childbearing and child-rearing redirect their ecstatic orientation away from the development of their own union and toward their family group. They find that family union is more meaningful than their own pairing and may devote themselves to experience that entity as fully as possible with their mate as a full role partner. For these individuals the dyad may fade into a unit serving their security needs while parenting and family life gain an ecstatic edge which does not diminish in importance even after children are less dependent and gone from the home. The role of grandparent may excite them as much as parenting did. They may end their lives together calling each other "grandma" and "grandpa," signifying their primary allegiance in both past and present. Other couples find that the work of raising children deepens the level of merger by allowing family allegiances to become a source of renewal without changing the dyadic focus.

Currently, there is no one cultural pattern to follow as a matter of course. Couples who are comfortable with traditional sex roles may find completeness in one another's functions, the man experiencing his nurturing capacities through her, the woman gratifying her aggressive impulses through him. They may feel a sense of sexual completion and wholeness in their reciprocal functions. Other couples may seek alternatives to traditional parenting roles. Both parents may want to live out all roles, moving beyond traditional distinctions to share both nurturing and acquisitive behaviors. They may even be able to merge their functions totally, husband and wife enmeshed in creating a total ambience of Parent which embraces the entire family. They are not necessarily sacrificing their own union or even their individuality for the "sake of the children." Rather they may continually be seeing themselves together renewing the dyad as the family passes through its shifting phases about them—adding to their experience but never diminishing their sense of pairing.

A couple must cooperatively establish a viable pattern. If they remain in conflict about roles and feelings, they will be burdened with confusion and dissonance. A couple with children who cannot use the family experience to renew their relationship and evolve a new level of sharing are faced with a difficult struggle if they are to keep their union ecstatic. Like the couple who remain childless, they must rely on inner resources and external techniques rather than sharing in the creative energies of the life cycle for renewal. But a couple with children must struggle to maintain their love commitment to each other in face of the time spent in and complexity of parenting roles and relationships. They are continually saddled with intruding, needful creatures and the conflicts that unwanted parenting roles produce.

The difficulty in finding sources for renewal within an ongoing love relationship goes beyond the presence or absence of children, other sources of interest, or even the commitment to one another. Renewal requires recognizing that the path is always open and the process of discovery without end. It is extremely difficult to risk what has been won and prized in the past. With adulthood also comes the process of aging, illness, and adjusting to losses. Increasingly with age, security may seem much more important than ever before. As with every ecstatic search, the movement toward each new level of merger risks all that has gone before. In the pursuit of a continuing ecstatic relationship, there can be no real stability, only a continued exploration of the Other.

A couple may begin to turn elsewhere when the ecstatic aspect of their relationship dims briefly. They may look for other paths outside their marriage. It is difficult to be honest with oneself or one's mate about the meaning of these diversions, especially since the same modes of heightening experience may serve either dyadic enrichment or escape. At critical decision points within relationships, that is, at times when the equilibrium can no longer remain stable, techniques can either renew or alienate. Marriage partners temporarily bored or disillusioned by their relationships may seek out together or alone one of the myriad opportunities for personal growth. They may believe that their goal is to bring their new awareness back to the marriage so that it can be revitalized and grow. But important growth experiences have their own pulls. They tend to draw persons inward to their own solitary world or submerge their identity in a group movement. Successful encounters with women's groups, group-relations conferences, Arica, Synanon games, and charismatic religious groups provide an ecstatic element in new form. The gain is in each person's new awareness of the capacity for rebirth; the risk is that the experience cannot be brought back to the dyad (if that was really the goal) but remains anchored in the new shell incommunicable to the Other and ultimately destructive to a union earlier thought to be worth preserving.

A common example is the dilemma of one member of a couple who attends a weekend marathon. The initial motivation may be to learn something more about interpersonal emotions, or "officially" to enhance professional competence, or simply to find excitement, but also with the thought of enriching a marriage or other ongoing relationship. The outcome of the weekend may be more meaningful than expected. The individual may experience significant personal insights and be moved to rapture by the "group high" that is the common subjective pathway of prolonged fatigue and catharsis in marathons. Ordinary life and relationships may seem dull and unrewarding in comparison. Returning for another weekend, that person may find himself once again drawn into the excitement, although he must exert more effort and commitment to reach the same heights now that the novelty is gone. Eventually he finds that he cannot participate in the encounter world as a visitor. He must adopt its social customs, study its ways, and embroil himself in its matrix or cease participation. What began as an educative experience may now threaten many previous assumptions about personal relationships. In fact that is what the group session was supposed to do; new feelings and insights can indeed be transferred to meaningful relationships in one's own life, such as a marital union. If a partner is open to exchanging and integrating even the most personal changes, then the weekend marathon could well become a renewing experience for a couple committed to ever deepening merger together. The work of transferring insights and emotions from one setting to another may seem hardly worth the trouble, especially if the group continues to offer ecstatic possibilities and the marital union is at a point where change is threatening. In such cases the experience may serve to divert the focus of meaning away from the hard work required of any long-term ecstatic commitment toward the more labile pleasures of "instant ecstasies."

The same kind of analysis applies to such renewal experiences as LSD, religious groups, and expanded sexual practices. Staying close to a safe routine that has worked in the past is not enough for relationships in which continuing ecstasy is sought. Like childbirth and parenting, all powerful renewing activities carry with them risks for the relationship's future. Any activity with an ecstatic potential outside of the ongoing dyad presents an alternate mode of experiencing merger which may inexorably lead away from the relationship. However, adults rarely change their ecstatic orientation completely. For that reason, most activities which committed couples use either to renew or disband their relationship remain connected to dyadic experience. New sexual practices are a common way in which couples attempt to revitalize the ecstatic elements of their marriage. They may go together to porno films or participate in sexual liaisons in which both share intimacies with the same person or a common group.

In the extreme, this may lead to a splitting off of ecstatic experience outside of marriage and dependency inside the marriage. The behavior of couples in "swinger" groups epitomizes this situation. For example, let us suppose that one of the partners has a problem at a swinger's party:

> It is expected that the other partner will take primary responsibility for doing what is necessary. One couple, for example, was at a gathering each sitting with their swinging partners. It was the first time they had ever tried pot, and the wife suddenly became hysterical. The man she was with quickly relinquished his place to her husband, who was expected to take primary responsibility for comforting his wife, although everyone was concerned about her. Another example can occur when a man has erection problems. If he is obviously miserable, it is considered wrong for his wife to ignore his condition, although we have heard of a few cases where this has happened. His wife may go to his side and they will decide to go home or she may simply act worried and less than completely enthusiastic, thus evincing some minimal concern for her husband. In other words, the married couple is still distinguished as the most compatible partners and remains therefore the primary problem solving unit.[3]

Many couples consciously enter these groups in an effort to renew a dying marriage, hoping that the new emotions developed out of the situation will somehow be transferred to their own union. They are rarely successful in their aim although most participants do experience a temporary heightening of their sexual pleasures with both their newer mates and their original partners. But rarely can these and similar experiences lead to a re-dedication to one another and a greater awareness of the need to cater to one another's sexual fantasies and pleasures rather than remain in older, more comfortable ways. Occasionally even the impersonal sex and sensuality doled out by professionals through prostitution or massage can reawaken needs and potentials that have lain dormant in a relationship which once included much more than child-rearing or financial security.

Couples who remain bound to one another through commitment to their dyad as their primary ecstatic form can and must be able to experiment in very profound ways together, alone, or in a group or family without losing one another to the experience. Without such freedom the dyad will become yet another prison for the self. There can be no real guarantees that in the course of an encounter in any one of these forms some insight or experience will not permanently damage the relationship; for not only would the guarantees be meaningless, but their existence would inevitably push the relationship toward dependence. There can be no restrictions on new experience and growth, not even on alternative dyadic love relationships, even though all lovers try to seek special guarantees from the Other. Here the love tradition is no different from other ecstatic traditions which seek to isolate their seekers from distracting bonds. Other traditions restrict relationships not so much because they fear the development of an ecstatic love bond in competition to their own ecstatic way, but because they fear the eroding power of dependency ties. For the love tradition, in which ecstatic relationships are the Way, the danger is far greater. Transient love affairs carry with them enormous attractions compared to longer-term commitment. Occasionally couples are able to use transient, passionate relationships with others to renew and enrich their own. But it is a rarity—the risks of destroying a long-term commitment are very great.

More usually, love affairs are used to supplement other relationships rather than to renew them. They can become a patterned way of life for the adult whose basic ecstatic orientation is dyadic but who does not have the concentration or perhaps the conviction to make a more total commitment in time as well as intensity. The experience is close to adolescent falling in love. Dependency and the emotions of permanence are separated from passionate liaison. Affairs are brief (or at least intermittent), soaring, and unburdened by promises and constraints. The forms of attraction are legion. Sometimes a particular body characteristic takes on the magnetism of a fetish. Dark hair, full body, reddish beard, special kinds of clothing, even a unique setting may trigger the experience, much like a Sufi chant induces a mystical experience or a post-hypnotic suggestion triggers a trance state. The experienced affair-seeker generally knows his own pattern and compulsively escapes from a relationship which might change it.

More threatening than affairs is the non-patterned and spontaneous act of falling deeply in love while still committed to another. Often the ongoing relationship has been in difficulty, perhaps overcome by a shared attempt at renewal. Often too some important life events have intervened to change the internal world of one of the partners, leaving the couple out of touch with each other. Sometimes a glimpse of merger shared with another as part of a group experience has broken an illusion of specialness or the experience of orgasm with another has diminished the magic of the original partner.

Whatever the reason, the fact of a new love experience competing with an old love relationship can precipitate the most painful kinds of re-evaluation which require great personal courage. It is difficult to act responsibly toward oneself in the face of societal and familial disapproval. Old relationships and old loyalties exert tremendous pressure against change and the fear of the unknown is pervasive.

In order to act there must also be self-knowledge, a grasp of what is possible, and an awareness of the limitation imposed by the past. Perhaps most challenging and disturbing of all to the Way of the ecstatic love tradition is the inexorable pressure of life events upon each of the parties and the union. Each new stage of development, each new rite of passage, each new crisis in daily living requires a new level of individual adjustment and a new level of merger. The old commitment to a love relationship must be redefined and recontained in each new form and the participants may lose their way. Either of the partners may leave, become ill, or die, leaving the other alone to struggle on a path which no longer exists. Other life challenges may temporarily dominate consciousness, a situation resulting in loneliness, isolation, and disillusion instead of rapture. The experience of living may itself feel meaningless as personal goals remain unfulfilled and the old relationships may be blamed. Seeking renewal within the dyad may become more and more difficult and new patterns may be sought.

Stereotypical escapes occur at each society's weakest points. In the seventies we are seeing an increase in thirty-year-old women leaving their children and hard-working husbands for the women's liberation movement. More traditionally, the middle-aged professional man leaves a warm and enduring marriage for a beautiful young woman. Occasionally an aging matron runs off with a young fortune seeker, leaving her husband and family in disarray. In these and thousands of other examples, the stress of social roles and personal difficulties forces the re-emergence of the dream of ecstatic experience. Instead of searching for new levels in the old relationships, individuals turn to new ones which may live up to their expectations, at least for a while. They decide that the hope of fulfillment is worth the risk of losing all their secure relationships.

More often, adults conceal their experience of profound emptiness. Couples often come to a psychiatrist or marriage counselor after the discovery of a surreptitious affair, in the face of persistent sexual failure, or when on the brink of realizing that the relationship is losing its roots. They are disturbed by a specific symptom and yet realize the meaninglessness of the general pattern. The counselor suggests that the partners need to work on their interactions over many months and at considerable expense, with no guarantee of success, in order to salvage the marriage. The barely recognized assumptions of many years may instantly be explicit. Is this relationship worth working for? Do I love my partner now? Can I give up casual affairs, business success, security? Am I willing to sacrifice my interests, my freedom, even my individual growth for the sake of this union? Is there another person who could satisfy my needs better? Is my ecstatic need better satisfied by other kinds of love relationships? Do I want to seek ecstasy through a long-term love relationship or is there a better way? Sidney Jourard echoes these questions when he lists the possibilities in a relationship which has become stale and habit-ridden:

> We may have to reexamine our projects, to see which have least meaning—our joint projects, or our singular projects. It may happen that we cannot invent or discover joint projects that infuse our life together with zest, and meaning, that we have to go separate ways. This becomes poignant if we are married, because we may decide—one, the other, or both—to become divorced. Or we may discover some new way to be married that looks like a "marriage of convenience"—no passion, not much delight, but some affection, trust, and goodwill. She might take a lover, I might take a mistress. That might be hurtful to all concerned, or perhaps not. If we have loved each other, and still do, the most loving thing to do might be to part, to dissolve the legal connection, and live separate lives with the hope of finding someone new to love.[4]

In the public domain, ecstatic experience in a marriage (or for that matter ecstatic experience in any mode) is hardly suitable to the work of living in society. The middle-aged professional who marries a young beauty and the housewife who leaves her children present a profound threat to their peers. What would happen to a society where great numbers of people acted on their passions? What if we all became "hedonists" or withdrew to the protection of a cloister or a monastery? The culture provides athletes, entertainers, and preachers as shamans and encourages us to revel in mysteries of ecstasy through their performance but not in our own lives. The public is shocked by those who dare to alter their life styles openly and seek ecstasy as a way of life. We expect it of our movie stars but not of our neighbors.

But adults have not lost their biological pleasure center nor the capacity for ecstatic experience. It may not be proper in most circles to quest quite so openly as the adolescent seeker or the members of fringe groups who have made that search into their life style; but the quest goes on nevertheless. It may be camouflaged in respectable summer travel, trips to the health club, or an arcane hobby. We are surprised to discover that a postal worker sniffs cocaine, that a prominent lawyer frequents erotic baths, or that a midwestern lady goes into trances during Sunday church service. But the potential is there in all of us, waiting for the right stimulus, for the release to be triggered.

Hindu tradition offers an institutionalized renewal of ecstatic experience by dividing life into four stages. This pattern reflects a larger metaphysic and a total ordering of society as well as of the personal life cycle. It enhances the sense of participating in a whole which transcends the "I." The first stage of initiation (at puberty) is that of student. A youth goes to live with his guru, to study scriptures, to learn control and ascetic principles and prepare for his adult responsibilities. In the second stage, the young man chooses a mate, marries, and becomes a householder. In this stage he is allowed sensual pleasures including sex, worldly involvement, and parenting. In the third stage, he returns to asceticism and the solitary mode:

> When a householder sees his skin wrinkled, and his hair white, and the sons of his sons, then he may resort to the forest.
>
> Abandoning all food raised by cultivation, and all his belongings, he may depart into the forest, either committing his wife to his sons, or accompanied by her.[5]

In the fourth stage, he becomes a homeless wanderer seeking final liberation:

> Let him always wander alone, without any companion, in order to attain final liberation, fully understanding that the solitary man, who neither forsakes nor is forsaken, gains his end.[6]

The ideal of the four stages is not realized in many cases. Nevertheless, it establishes a pattern of stages in which one is permitted to be involved in worldly entanglements. Involvement in the life cycle and in sensual pleasure is valued as long as it is indulged at the appropriate time. The ascetic ideal of ecstasy is reserved for the stage beyond the birth cycle when the renewal of marriage and parenting have ended.

Earlier societies have rarely had to concern themselves with many alternate life roles beyond those encompassing the birth cycle. Before modern public medicine, relatively few people lived into advanced years and those who did were welcomed as sages and seers. Our culture is in a radically different position. When we come to the end of our "householder" responsibilities, when we pass beyond the birth cycle, we still have half of our lives before us. We have not established special roles for the middle-aged, for the retired, nor have we any assumptions about their ecstatic quest. Perhaps the Hindus evolved their system of sending the elderly off as hermits in order to present the next generation with an opportunity to exercise power and responsibility. Whatever the motive, the Hindus also defined relationships and worldly ties as inhibiting to "liberation" or to transcendence of the ego. The pattern implies that the individual must inevitably progress toward increasing solitude and finally give up even the dyad.

The experience of life for many adults is of increasing sense of loss. The parents and friends of childhood, the community of youth, the familiar life style learned in the earliest years, slowly slip away. More and more friends and relatives disappear, dead or out of touch. Many adults choose to move into an isolated style as self-protection, that is, in order to save the "I" from the pain of more loss. They may be hesitant to make new attachments and become involved in new relationships that may also result in loss. Furthermore, they may be weary of the perpetual need to explain their lives to younger people who share none of their basic assumptions. They may feel a profound need for an Other who knows how they feel or what they mean without an explanation. Solitary and group modalities may become more acceptable than dyadic encounters. In middle age, many adults throw themselves into a more youthful style, desperately trying to forget all that has passed. Such techniques become increasingly difficult as the years advance. In extreme old age, there are those who can be seen to have withdrawn almost totally into a dream world in which fantasies of people long dead are more real than the presence of people still living.

There is some evidence that many people prefer to be free of their entangling relationships and uninhibited by "love" ties as they confront death. Elisabeth Kubler-Ross has developed five stages of dying which she sees as a normal progression in the terminally ill. In the final stage, which is acceptance, relationships with loved ones become complicated and ambivalent affairs. The person wants to be left alone, to become increasingly detached from life, while readying himself for departure. The spouse or parent or other lover to be left behind may not be able to accept this increasing aloofness and may try to hold on, as in the following case history:

> She felt strongly that her life, especially her marriage, had been a good and meaningful one and that there was little left that she could do. She asked to be allowed to die in peace, wished to be left alone—even asked for less involvement on the part of her husband. She said that the only reason that kept her still alive was her husband's inability to accept the fact that she had to die. She was angry at him for not facing it and for so desperately clinging on to something that she was willing and ready to give up. I translated to her that she wished to detach herself from this world and she nodded gratefully as I left her alone.[7]

This is not to say that relationships become meaningless—rather that they become a burden and an intrusion to someone in an essentially isolated experience. There are many other people who want their loved ones with them to the end. Here, as at every point in the life cycle, ecstatic orientation is reflected in the needs of the individual. The member of a religious sect or extraordinarily close-knit community might feel most secure when surrounded by representatives of the community. Dying adolescents are particularly apt to wish to have others with them. In cases of strong dyadic orientation, a dying partner may be comfortable only when in actual physical contact with the Other. He may experience himself dissolving into the Other while sensing that his life is not totally ending as long as his mate or his offspring continue.

The dying person wants to feel that his responsibilities and obligations are over and that his loved ones understand and accept his departure. The greater problem exists for the one who is left behind. He must watch his beloved move inexorably away from him, become detached and withdrawn, accepting of the inevitable separation. The loss of the other half of a dyad is perhaps harder to face than death itself and yet both are inevitable in human existence. The pain, however, does not preclude ecstatic experience, as the following poem by Tagore suggests:

> *In desperate hope I go and search for her in all the corners of my room; I find her not.*
>
> *My house is small and what once has gone from it can never be regained.*
>
> *But infinite is thy mansion, my lord, and seeking her I have come to thy door.*
>
> *I stand under the golden canopy of thine evening sky and I lift my eager eyes to thy face.*
>
> *I have come to the brink of eternity from which nothing can vanish—no hope, no happiness, no vision of a face seen through tears.*
>
> *Oh, dip my emptied life into that ocean, plunge it into the deepest fullness. Let me for once feel that lost sweet touch in the allness of the universe.**

Death is frequently described as an experience of union. As body functions cease, individual boundaries and the sense of "I" disintegrate or lapse into meaninglessness. As in other altered

* From "Gitanjali," LXXXVII, from *Collected Poems and Plays* by Rabindranath Tagore, published in the United States by Macmillan Publishing Co., Inc., 1913. Reprinted by permission of Macmillan Publishing Co., Inc.

states of consciousness, the experience may be frightening or exquisite. Ecstasy pushes beyond the "I" but is shaped by individual patterns and personal interpretations. Death, like puberty, birth, and marriage, can be shaped by circumstance. At its best, the ecstatic orientation of the dying person is taken into account as the caring parties provide for fundamental physical and psychological needs.

As ageless traditions of mystical experience and such modern scholars as Maslow and Buber remind us, there is much more to our natures than combatting fear and pain, more to love than need and dependence. The human ecstatic potential can at times transcend dependency needs even while reducing the pain of isolation. There is no loneliness at the most sacred heights of ecstatic experience where identity and cosmic unity are one and the same. Just as the experience of absolute, joyous comfort defines a state of bliss, so the fusion of dependency and ecstasy in a relationship is the fusion of all opposites in the unity experience. It is a fusion which extends beyond that part of our psychology which *needs* rather than *is*. Such experiences as "falling in love," ecstatic friendship, or sexual symbiosis are described by such a fusion. The pervasive fear of loss is momentarily overcome in the timeless space where ecstatic experience occurs. It is really only in this fusion which is the essence of all ecstasies (including love) that dependency in relationships is overcome.

There is a critical distinction between the universality of love and the particularity of an ecstatic love tradition. The forms that we use to reach our particular ecstatic goals depend on our orientation—whether to totality, dyad, group, heightened "I," or the infinite combination of these and other factors yet unnamed which affect how we seek and find ecstasy. Over a period of time, the love experience tends to blend with many feelings such as caring, security, the acts through which the loneliness is muted and absorbed. These emotions may begin by enhancing the love relationship and end by becoming its center to the exclusion of the more labile ecstatic edge of experience. They may eventually take over as the dominant qualities of the relationship. Some couples learn how to move beyond the first few ecstatic experiences and structure their lives toward a continuing search for "enormous bliss." Almost all of us fall in love, but only a few of us will continue to see relationships as the prime medium for ecstatic expression and choose to live out our lives together with another in pursuit of that mystical quest.

What does living together in ecstasy mean? What would it be like to encounter one's mate on the high plateau of ecstatic love day after day, year after year—so that, in Buber's words, "I require a You to become I, becoming I, I say you"? [8] It goes beyond a "good" marriage or a supportful union; it goes beyond a relationship in which both individuals are helped to grow to their full potential. It is an ecstatic union, one in which the merger with the other and loss of "I"-ness is at once an ongoing experience and the highest goal of the pair. It is a relationship in which the union of sex and orgasm are an essence and a metaphor for all shared acts together, when experience is joined and consciousness united.

Love, in the particularity of an ecstatic tradition, is not simply the serial continuation of the instant ecstasy of falling in love. Beyond orientation and commitment to ecstasy with another is a way-of-being-in-the-relationship so that the ordinary transactions of the day-to-day world are also innumerable bridges to the extraordinary universe of transcendent emotion. Ecstatic relating requires the development of an ongoing awareness of the symbol behind each action and the potential merger through each shared symbol. It is not unique to the love experience. It is often described as the glow after an ecstatic peak when sublime meaning surrounds even the most simple events, or as a "plateau experience" which involves seeing the transcendent as part of the real world.

In the long-term dyad, lovers would share a vision of the world in which the ordinary was also extraordinary. The sense of real merger with the Other would be the center of consciousness for both. The ordinary sense of partnership and participation in common life tasks reflects the profound consciousness of merger, of loss of individual identity in a duality which is a larger unity. The work of achieving this potentiality requires not only preparing the mind for the loss of individuality but nurturing a commitment to a relationship capable of sustaining ecstatic moments as a way of life.

8

The Ecstasy of Love

WE have defined love as both a feeling and a way of relating, an emotion and a human interaction. It is conceptualized as the intersection of two dimensions of human process. One dimension contains the quest for ecstatic experiences which haunts man from the first moment he tastes the exquisite sensations of "oneness" or "wholeness." The other dimension contains the world of interpersonal relationships which dominate experience throughout life.

The dimension of ecstasy and the dimension of relationships do not intersect easily or often. Ecstatic experience may be represented by a single figure, facing the world and the self in magnificent aloneness: the burning frenzy of the possessed scholar in search of truth; the devout holy man in communion with self; the visionary prophet at one with his fantasy; even the hedonist with his multitude of sensual pleasures; none of them is with an Other. In their quest they often require teachers and guides and helpmates; but eventually they travel alone. The tradition of yoga speaks of "purification," warning again and again against the intrusion of relationships, even of the "subconscious" remnants of attachment to the "I." Most ecstatic traditions label close personal relationships an impediment in the quest toward expanding the germ of ecstasy in oneself.

It is easy to see why human relationships are excluded from the ecstatic quest. The choice between accepting ourselves as self-sufficient and reaching out to another is an eternal conflict defining each individual's balance between acceptance of existential isolation and perseverance in achieving union with others. It is as difficult to be alone as it is to be intimate. Often it seems as though the quest for ecstasy begins as an escape from the dangers of human relationship, that is, an attempt to flee the intricate tortures men and women concoct for those they know intimately.

Yet there is the potential of love, the hope of finding ecstasy in human relationships, of transcending mundane squabbles and discovering mutual joy. Whenever ecstasy is experienced in the developing closeness between two people, they speak of it as love. The intense soaring quality of "falling" in love, the unimagined pleasure of revealing the emotions of self to another, the sexual delights given and received, the serenity of being together, trusting, becoming one and separating, the mutual cosmic creation of another in pregnancy, childbirth, and parenting—to catalogue the ecstatic moments in the history of a relationship is to trace the thread of love between two people.

Love is ecstasy in a relationship. It is not an easy way to describe love, for most relationships do not support ecstatic experience. But love is undeniable. The comforts of a stable, socially appropriate relationship which satisfies the needs for dependence is not the same as ecstasy. Ecstatic moments can be temporarily forgotten or repressed. Ecstatic experience can be sought outside of relationships. But almost inevitably the stab of ecstasy is re-experienced in a new relationship with another person. Because love is so intense it will be sought again and again. Marriages and other partnerships may be jeopardized; family loyalties, even basic sexual identity, may be altered in the pursuit of ecstatic love. Entire political systems have been ravaged by the sudden rush of love affecting a critical leader or alliance. The saying that "all the world loves a lover" is patently false. Love is the enemy of order and ritual. If ecstasy can be removed from the context of a relationship and transferred to God, body, or inner vision, then impulses toward disorder have been brought under control. Society breathes more freely.

Love is as threatening for the individual as for the culture. Relationships offer far more than ecstasy. They offer security, a stable base from which to pursue other life goals. They offer the opportunity to mitigate the ever present sense of isolation. And more perversely, relationships offer a place to indulge in the endless fantasies that are the unfinished part of every childhood, the scripts, the games, the past pleasures that can be recapitulated in a variety of disguises. It is difficult to set such pleasures aside even when the total form of the relationship is a nightmare. The risk is great since even the most pathological liaisons may serve the quest. The sadist who is beaten by another to the accompaniment of his own autistic fantasies is structuring a distorted human dyad to serve a hidden need. The ecstasy of pain/pleasure is only a peripheral aspect of a relationship. The hand that holds the whip is interchangeable. This way of relating with others strains even the most non-demanding definitions of human interactions. Yet once an ecstatic orientation is fixed, it is incredibly difficult to change directions. It is like asking the dedicated yogi to abandon his discipline or the monk who has found God to enter a human relationship. Human love is not an easy Way to find fulfillment. It is a Way, but not the only way.

All ecstatic traditions require an enduring commitment. Love is no exception. It may be the most rigorous of all because it requires more than *self*-discipline. It requires trust in the fidelity of another. It is like meditating on an unfixed point, a pattern which may move or change or disintegrate at any moment. It is like meditating on a poem in composition; it is as unstable as the novice's ability to fix his attention. It is like trying to lose his sense of "I" on a seesaw with another. It is like trying to encompass the universe when the universe walks and talks and makes love. It is like trying to lose oneself in an orgasm when the Other may withdraw unsatisfied. Love offers little hope of fulfillment and yet it is the standard of all ecstasies and all ecstatic traditions.

In the beginning the infant does not know of his own existence as something separate and apart from the world around him. It is only gradually that his merger with totality is replaced by a merger with his mother and later the people in his environment. The infant experiences intense pleasure, even ecstasy, before his relationships with others are forged. That experience is identity-less, pleasure experienced as a part merged with a whole. It goes beyond one's animal origins to a total union with the universe. Here is the model for ecstasy with loss of "I," for total union, for the final liberation. It is sleep without dreams, with no vestige of differentiation, a time and a consciousness before the egg and sperm divided, before life began.

The ecstasy of love derives from a later pre-relational state, the infant's experience of his own merger with another human. Within the extraordinary emotions provided by the original symbiotic dyad lies the kernel of the love experience. In this dyad a pre-emergent "I" glimpses his core human identity as more than an object and evolves his first assumptions about personhood and relating.

Love is revelling in humanness. It pulls us back from the molecular stream and calls attention to our special place in the universe. It differs from other forms of ecstasy in which personhood is yet another encumbrance, another layer to shed on the way toward the ultimate nothingness which is unity with everything. Its aim is the most total awareness of our special place in the universe of matter. Its form is the dyad because there is no more profound way to acknowledge our human bonds. The ecstasy of love is the final assertion of being human.

Notes

Chapter 1. A Definition of Love

1. Erich Fromm, *The Art of Loving: An Enquiry into the Nature of Love* (New York: Harper & Row, 1956).

Chapter 2. The Experience of Ecstasy

1. The term "transpersonal psychology" has been chosen as the title of a journal begun in 1971 to explore psychological conditions that would generally be called ecstatic, mystical, or freaked-out by the layman.

2. William James, *The Varieties of Religious Experience* (Garden City, N.Y.: Doubleday, 1902), p. 349.

3. Mircea Eliade, *Yoga: Immortality and Freedom,* translated by Willard Trask (Princeton: Princeton University Press, 1969), p. 55.

4. Plato, "The Symposium," in *The Works of Plato,* selected and edited by Irwin Edman (New York: Random House, 1956), p. 337.

5. Mircea Eliade, *The Two and The One,* translated by J. M. Cohen (New York: Harper & Row, 1965), p. 138.

6. R. Gordon Wasson, "The Divine Mushroom of Immortality," in *The Flesh of the Gods,* edited by Peter T. Furst (New York: Praeger, 1972), p. 199.

7. *Psychiatric Dictionary,* Third Edition, edited by Leland E. Hinsie, M.D. and Robert Jean Campbell, M.D. (New York: Oxford University Press, 1960), p. 244.

8. See, for example, P. C. Horton, "The Mystical Experience as a Suicide Preventive," *American Journal of Psychiatry,* 130 (1973), 294–296.

9. J. W. Perry, "Reconstitutive Process in the Psychopathology of the Self," *Annals of New York Academy of Sciences,* XCVI (1962), 853–876.

10. Abraham H. Maslow, *Religions, Values, and Peak-Experiences* (New York: The Viking Press, 1970), p. 22.

11. *Ibid.,* pp. 22–23.

12. D. H. Lawrence, *Women in Love* (New York: Random House, 1950), p. 307.

13. Omar Garrison, *Tantra: The Yoga of Sex* (New York: The Julian Press, 1964), pp. 114–115.

14. Stanislav Grof, "Beyond the Bounds of Psychoanalysis," *Intellectual Digest* (September 1972), 86–88.

15. St. Teresa of Avila, "Of the Fourth Degree of Prayer," quoted in F. C. Happold, *Mysticism: A Study and an Anthology* (Baltimore: Penguin Books, 1964), pp. 321–323.

16. Timothy Leary, Ralph Metzner, and Richard Alpert, *The Psychedelic Experience: A Manual Based on the Tibetan Book of the Dead* (New York: University Books, 1964).

17. Jose R. Delgado, M.D., *Physical Control of the Mind: Toward a Psychocivilized Society* (New York: Harper & Row, 1969), p. 62.

18. John Lilly, *The Center of the Cyclone: An Autobiography of Inner Space* (New York: The Julian Press, 1972), pp. 42–43. Italics ours.

19. One of us (A.C.) observed experiments of this kind as a medical student. The subjects were consistently warned about the frightening things they would face during the experiment. Many of them began describing pleasant mental alterations but invariably the more frightening and "psychotic-like" observations were the ones to be reinforced.

20. Delgado, *op. cit.,* p. 574.

21. R. G. Heath, "Electric Self-Stimulation in the Brain in Man," *American Journal of Psychiatry* (1963), 571–577.

22. R. G. Heath, "Marijuana: Effects on Deep and Surface Electroencephalograms," *Archives of General Psychiatry,* XXVI (1972), 577–584.

23. Delgado, *op. cit.,* p. 146.

24. Leary, *et al., op. cit.,* p. 36.

25. Farid al-din 'Attar, translated by Margaret Smith in Happold, *op. cit.,* p. 227.

26. Robert E. Ornstein, *On the Psychology of Meditation* (New York: The Viking Press, 1972), p. 169.

27. Lilly, *op. cit.,* p. 109.

28. Arthur J. Deikman, "Experimental Meditation," *Journal of Nervous and Mental Disorders,* vol. 136, 329–373.

29. Ornstein, *op. cit.,* p. 196.

30. From the Tao T. Ching, quoted by Houston Smith in *The Religions of Man* (New York: The New American Library, 1959), p. 191.

31. Quoted by William James, *op. cit.,* p. 346.

32. Sita Wiener, *Swami Satchidananda* (New York: Bantam Books, 1972), p. 4.

33. Plato, *op. cit.,* p. 291.

34. Happold, *op. cit.,* pp. 322–323.

35. W. G. Archer, *The Loves of Krishna* (New York: Grove Press), p. 43.

36. Wiener, *op. cit.,* p. 79.

37. W. R. Bion, *Experiences in Groups* (New York: Basic Books, 1959).

38. James W. Fernandez, "*Tabernanthe Iboga:* Narcotic Ecstasis and the Work of the Ancestors," in Furst, *op. cit.,* p. 240.

39. I. M. Lewis, *Ecstatic Religions: An Anthropological Study of Spirit Possession and Shamanism* (Baltimore: Penguin Books, 1971), p. 53.

40. R. Gordon Wasson, "What Was the Soma of the Aryans?" in Furst, *op. cit.,* pp. 201–213. See also Weston La Barred, "Hallucinogens and the Shamanistic Origins of Religion," in the same volume, pp. 261–278.

Chapter 3. The Dyad in Ecstatic Traditions

1. C. S. Lewis, *Surprised by Joy: The Shape of My Early Life* (New York: Harcourt Brace & World, 1955), p. 18.

2. Betty Kelen, *Gautama Buddha in Life and Legend* (New York: Avon, 1967), pp. 35–36.

3. Carlos Castaneda, *A Separate Reality: Further Conversations with Don Juan* (New York: Simon and Schuster, 1971).

4. Fernandez, *op. cit.,* pp. 251–252.

5. Wiener, *op. cit.,* p. 35.

6. P. D. Ouspensky, *In Search of the Miraculous* (New York: Harcourt, Brace & World, 1949), p. 59.

7. Sheldon Kopp, *Guru* (Palo Alto: Science & Behavior Books, 1971).

8. William Shakespeare, *A Midsummer Night's Dream,* V, i.

9. Martin Buber, *I and Thou,* transl. by Walter Kaufman (New York: Charles Scribner's Sons, 1970), p. 126.

10. *The Kama Sutra of Vatsyayana,* Foreword by Santha Rama Rau, Introduction by John W. Spellman (New York: E. P. Dutton & Co., 1964), pp. 41–42.

11. Garrison, *op. cit.*, p. 112.
12. *Ibid.*, p. 114.
13. *Ibid.*, p. 207.
14. Plato, *op. cit.*, p. 194.
15. Denis de Rougemont, *Love in the Western World*, translated by Montgomery Belgion (New York: Random House, 1956).
16. *Ibid.*, p. 34.
17. Buber, *op. cit.*, p. 54.
18. *Ibid.*, p. 95.

Chapter 4. The Origin of Ecstatic Consciousness (Pre-Relational Stages of Development)

1. Sigmund Freud, "Civilization and Its Discontents," in *The Standard Edition of Sigmund Freud*, Vol. XXI, pp. 59–145.
2. Carl Jung, *Psychology of the Unconscious* (London: Routledge and Kegan Paul, 1919), pp. 198–199.
3. Libby and Arthur Colman, "Pregnancy as an Altered State of Consciousness," *Birth and the Family Journal*, I (1973), 7–11.
4. Marshall Klaus, *et al.*, "Maternal Attachment: Importance of the First Post-Partum Days," *New England Journal of Medicine*, (1972), 286–296.
5. M. S. Mahler, "On the First Three Subphases of the Separation-Individuation Process," *International Journal of Psychoanalysis, 53 (1972), 333*–338.
6. Selma H. Freiberg, *The Magic Years: Understanding and Handling the Problems of Early Childhood* (New York: Charles Scribner's Sons, 1959), p. 37.
7. W. G. Joffe and J. Sandler, "Notes on Pain, Depression and Individuation," *Psychoanalytic Study of the Child*, 20 (1965), 394–424.

Chapter 5. The Development of Ecstatic Relationships in Childhood

1. Robert C. O'Brien, *The Silver Crown* (New York: Atheneum, 1968), p. 150.
2. Erich Fromm, *op. cit.*, p. 40.
3. H. S. Sullivan, *The Interpersonal Theory of Psychiatry* (New York: W. W. Norton & Co., 1953).
4. Erik Erikson, *Childhood and Society*, Second Edition (New York: W. W. Norton & Co., 1963).
5. Arthur and Libby Colman, "Psychological Complications of Pregnancy," in *Toward a Better Beginning* (Tacoma: Childbirth

Education Association of Tacoma, 1973), pp. 122–133; and *Pregnancy: The Psychological Experience* (New York: The Seabury Press, 1971).

6. Joseph Chilton Pearce, *Crack in the Cosmic Egg* (New York: Pocket Books, 1973), pp. 29–30.

7. "Interview: Eileen J. Garrett," *Psychic* (May/June 1970), 6.

8. "Interview: Ingo Swann," *Psychic* (March/April 1973), 8.

9. Richard Noone with Dennis Holman, *In Search of the Dream People* (New York: William Morrow & Co., 1972).

Chapter 6. Ecstatic Relationships in Adolescence

1. Ouspensky, *op. cit.*

2. Mircea Eliade, *The Sacred and the Profane: The Nature of Religion,* translated by Willard R. Trask (New York: Harcourt, Brace & World, 1959).

3. *The Compact Edition of the Oxford English Dictionary* (Oxford: Clarendon Press, 1971), p. 2349.

4. *Ibid.,* p. 31.

5. Garrison, *op. cit.,* pp. 94–95.

6. Quoted by Norman Kiell in *The Universal Experience of Adolescence* (New York: International Universities Press, 1964), p. 144.

7. *Ibid.,* p. 186.

8. Marguerite Duras, *The Ravishing of Lol Stein,* transl. by Richard Seaver (New York: Grove Press, 1966).

9. Michael Gall, "Afterword," in Lowell Blair, *Eros and Psyche,* translated by Alexis Socratos (Berkeley: Berkeley Publishing Corp., 1972), pp. 153–160.

10. C. S. Lewis, *The Four Loves* (New York: Harcourt Brace Jovanovich, Inc., 1960), p. 88.

11. Erik Erikson, "Identity and the Life Cycle," *Psychological Issues* I, (1959), p. 95.

Chapter 7. Adult Love

1. Orson Bean, *Me and the Orgone,* With an Introduction by A. S. Neill (New York: St. Martin Press, 1971), p. 13.

2. Plato, *op. cit.,* p. 375.

3. Charles and Rebecca Palson, "Swinging in Wedlock," *Society (Transaction),* 1972.

4. Sidney Jourard, "Some Dimensions of Loving Experience," in Herbert A. Otto (editor), *Love Today: A New Exploration* (New York: Dell, 1972), p. 47.

5. Ainslie T. Embree, editor, *The Hindu Tradition: Readings in Oriental Thought* (New York: Random House, 1972), pp. 90–91.

6. *Ibid.*, p. 92.

7. E. K. Ross, *On Death and Dying* (New York: Macmillan, 1969), p. 148.

8. Buber, *Op. cit.*, p. 68.

Arthur D. Colman, BA Harvard '58, MD Harvard '62, is Associate Clinical Professor at the University of California Medical Center in San Francisco. He spends much of his time writing and in the private practice of psychiatry. He is a frequent contributor to professional journals and author of a book on psychiatric ward design. **Libby Lee Colman,** BA Wellesley '62, PhD (in English literature) George Washington University '72, teaches part-time. The Colmans co-authored an earlier book, *Pregnancy: The Psychological Experience.* They live with their three children and three dogs in the Bay area.